Office of Arts and Libraries

Volunteers in Museums and Heritage Organisations

Policy, Planning and Management

with a foreword from
The Rt Hon Tim Renton MP
Minister for the Arts

London: HMSO

© Crown copyright 1991
First published 1991

British Library Cataloguing in Publication Data

A CIP catalogue record for this book is available
from the British Library

ISBN 0 11 290491 2

HMSO publications are available from:

HMSO Publications Centre
(Mail and telephone orders only)
PO Box 276, London, SW8 5DT
Telephone orders 071-873 9090
General enquiries 071-873 0011
(queuing system in operation for both numbers)

HMSO Bookshops
49 High Holborn, London, WC1V 6HB   071-873 0011
(counter service only)
258 Broad Street, Birmingham, B1 2HE   021-643 3740
Southey House, 33 Wine Street, Bristol, BS1 2BQ   (0272)
264306
9–21 Princess Street, Manchester, M60 8AS   061-834 7201
80 Chichester Street, Belfast, BT1 4JY   (0232) 238451
71 Lothian Road, Edinburgh, EH3 9AZ   031-228 4181

HMSO's Accredited Agents
(see Yellow Pages)

and through good booksellers

Printed in the United Kingdom for HMSO
Dd 292026 5/91 C16

Contents

Project Director and written by:

Sue Millar, BA, MA, Lecturer in Heritage Management, University of Birmingham. Currently Head of Education, National Maritime Museum

Research Officer:

Janet Wassall, BA, Research Associate, University of Birmingham.

Steering Committee Members:

Nigel Pittman, Chairman, Head of Museums and Galleries Division, Office of Arts and Libraries. (Sandra Brown until November 1989)
Margaret Beard, Chairman, NADFAS Volunteers
Michael Diamond, Director, Birmingham City Museum and Art Gallery
Rosemary Ewles, Museums Officer, Museums and Galleries Commission
Dr Patrick Greene, Director, Museum of Science and Industry, Manchester
Michaela Jenkerson-Kenshole, Chairman (until April 1989), NADFAS Volunteers
Gillian Lewis, Head of Conservation, National Maritime Museum
Rosemary Marsh, Chairman, British Association of Friends of Museums
Leslie McCracken, Deputy Secretary, The National Trust
Roger Watkins, Consultant, Voluntary Services Unit, Home Office
Elaine Willis, Deputy Director, The Volunteer Centre UK.

OAL Support:

Ian Baxter, Sharon Cannon & William Barker

Acknowledgements:

We should like to thank those museums throughout the United Kingdom, Italy and the United States which have contributed to this publication. The unstinting and willing efforts of people within these organisations—paid staff and volunteers alike—means that an impressive and extensive amount of research data has been amassed in the form of written evidence, personal interviews and case studies. The assistance of other heritage bodies such as the National Trust has been invaluable. Thanks are also due to members of the voluntary societies connected to museums—BAFM, NADFAS and VAMI—and the Volunteer Centre UK. The support of the Ironbridge Institute and the Dean of the Faculty of Commerce and Social Science, University of Birmingham, facilitated, firstly, the commencement and, secondly, the completion of the project. Funding from the Office of Arts and Libraries has enabled this study to have an international focus and to be both a wide ranging and an in-depth investigation into good practice in the management of volunteers in museums and heritage organisations.

Note:

The word 'museum' is used throughout this publication to denote 'museum and gallery'.

Foreword

Policy planning and good management are essential to the well-being of all museums. Indeed, the degree of success achieved by large, publicly funded museums and the very survival of many small, independent museums depends on the careful planning of expenditure and the ability to maximise the use of available resources—including the services of volunteers.

Volunteers do not replace paid staff but, if properly managed, they can increase effectiveness by making available additional resources of help and skill.

Volunteer involvement and volunteer enthusiasm have the potential to improve every aspect of museums, provide opportunities to pilot new projects and engender strong links between the museum and the community. Much good practice already exists and volunteers offer support to museums in numerous ways. They are active in all areas of museum work and at every level in museums' management.

The challenge for museums is how to involve volunteers creatively and effectively in future developments and new initiatives. The Museum Registration Scheme should bring volunteers and all-volunteer museums within the museum community and will stress the need for high standards. The Office of Arts and Libraries and the Museums and Galleries Commission are keen to encourage good management practice so that the full potential of volunteers can be realised.

The aim of this publication is to provide museums' governing bodies, directors, curators and other museum staff with practical help and advice on the management of volunteers. For entirely volunteer-run museums it will assist in the process of self-management. An overview of the nature of volunteering in museums in the United Kingdom gives a context for policy planning. However, this is primarily a practical guide to inform decisions about placing volunteers within different organisational structures, to offer guidance on procedures for recruiting and retaining volunteers and to present the legal aspects of volunteer involvement. Case studies give detailed examples of good practice. Research for this publication was extensive and included an international perspective with visits to museums in the United States and Italy.

The Office of Arts and Libraries and the Museum and Galleries Commission have a common interest in promoting the partnership between museums and volunteers. At a time when museums are reviewing all aspects of their planning and management and decisions are being made which will shape their long-term future, the opportunities are immense. As a contribution to this process, I strongly commend this publication to all involved in the running of museums.

Tim Renton, MP
Minister for the Arts

1 Introduction

Aims and Objectives

Volunteers are a significant part of the museum community. Volunteers are the ultimate frequent visitors. The growth of museums at the rate of one a fortnight in recent years is due mainly to the huge growth in voluntary trusts and 'all volunteer' museums. Yet, in the current debate on the function of museums in society the place of volunteers in museums merits scarcely a mention. It is important to redress the balance.

Museums will be competing for people in the labour market of the 1990s—especially those people who have skills and expertise to offer. An expected increase in demand for volunteers across the fields of cultural and social services comes at a time when traditional sources of volunteer supply are shrinking. Demographic trends show that there will be a dramatic decrease in the number of 16–19 year olds throughout Europe. Their number will fall by 25% by 1995. There will be a 'middle age bulge' by the year 2000 with an older working population in the age range 40–64 years.

Volunteer policy planning and the management of volunteer programmes is a major area of development that museums in the United Kingdom must address over the next decade. *Volunteers in Museums and Heritage Organisations: Policy Planning and Management* examines the place of the volunteer contribution to National, Local Authority and Independent Museums in the immediate context of corporate planning within museums, on the one hand, and in the broader context of voluntary activity in the 1990s, on the other.

Practical advice is offered to all museums and heritage organisations on policy planning, questions concerning volunteer co-ordinators, recruitment, induction and training as well as such mundane, but essential issues as employment law and liability and the complexities of working relations when paid staff work alongside volunteers. Throughout, there is an emphasis on designing effective management policies based on examples of good practice. In general, museums in the United Kingdom have no written guidelines or directives as part of an overall management strategy on staffing resources. The few guidelines that do exist exhibit creative management thinking and represent the first tentative steps in this direction. In the United States, guidelines in the form of handbooks giving details on the practices and procedures relating to the employment of volunteers, are more common.

Good practice is not to be equated with standardisation and *Volunteers in Museums and Heritage Organisations: Policy Planning and Management* addresses the intricacies of volunteer management within museums. Understanding what others have achieved and how they have achieved it, however, enables a cross-fertilization of ideas that helps museums to overcome the isolation and insularity they can otherwise face. Each museum is unique. The purpose of this publication is to assist each one to plan its own volunteer policy, establish practices and procedures, and design appropriate and imaginative volunteer programmes that are tailor-made to suit the needs of individual circumstances. Excellent schemes are in operation across the range of museum activities and these are outlined in the case studies.

Research and Methodology

Research undertaken within the United Kingdom, the USA and Italy over the past year has revealed the breadth and depth of the volunteer contribution to the well-being of all museums. It has shown the immense scope and variety of the contributions from people who give their time freely at different levels within the management structure, in different ways and with different degrees of recognition. Volunteers are present and actively involved in all aspects of museum work including collections management—conservation, documentation and research; access to collections—exhibitions, education, interpretation, information, security, marketing and public relations and in support roles such as fund-raising and administration.

Volunteers are also present as museum committee members, trustees and members of governing bodies. The focus of this study, however, is on the day to day management of volunteers either by paid staff or by other volunteers, the organisation of internships, the place of associations of Friends and other groups such as NADFAS. Whereas Boards of Trustees and other governing bodies are acknowledged as an area of major importance in terms of voluntary activity within museums in the United Kingdom, the specific issues that relate to them are seen as beyond the remit of this project and worthy of separate attention. A code of practice for museum committee members, trustees and members of governing bodies originally prepared by the Chairman of the Scottish Museums Council, 'to provide something that tell us what to do since we hold the public's collection in trust,' was approved by the Museums Association's conference in July 1990.

From the outset, a qualitative rather than a quantitative approach to research was taken. The purpose was to find out exactly what was the nature of volunteer activity in museums and to highlight good practice in order that this publication was not just another set of management principles. If lip-service to the inclusion of volunteers in staffing policies is to be avoided and planning and management are to be instrumental in effecting real change in the practice of managing volunteers in museums and heritage organisations, then a close association between theory and practice is essential. The management structures of museums in the United Kingdom are as many and varied as their different sizes, origins, locations, aims and objectives. This publication takes account of this situation.

In England, Scotland, Wales and Northern Ireland information has been gathered through seeking written or telephone replies to a *Statement of Intent* that was circulated to museums and heritage organisations during the Summer, 1989. The response and support for the project was overwhelming and confirmed the need for a publication on volunteer policy planning and management. A large sample of museums and heritage organisations throughout the United Kingdom were selected for visits and interviews with paid staff and volunteers. These interviews provided a subtle insight into what is happening on the ground.

The lack of centralised co-ordination of volunteer activity—or even a volunteer co-ordinator—in many large publicly funded museums means that only by talking to people on site has it been possible to discover the wide range of ways volunteers give their time and skills to a museum or heritage organisation. This contrasts with the situation in the United States where it is more general for paid staff to be appointed to organise volunteers and contact was easy. Italy is different again. Meetings were arranged with VAMI since all volunteer activity is organised exclusively by this outside body. Friends Associations in the United Kingdom, responsible for organising practical assistance, were also consulted.

There is an overwhelming amount of volunteer activity in museums throughout the United Kingdom. The importance of this activity both in terms of the accountability of the museum to the community of which it is a part and in terms of the direct and indirect contribution of volunteers to the financial accountability of the museum is addressed in the context chapter.

The Relationship of Museums to the Voluntary Sector

There is an over-arching grey area where a museum, be it National, Local Authority or Independent, fuses with the community. There is a two way sense of belonging. There are two way benefits. Participation by individuals from the community through active citizenship gives that community an increased sense of ownership of the museum. For museums, volunteer labour, expertise and influence in the community represent a financial asset rarely recognised in financial management strategies and business plans, except in the case of mainly voluntary independent museums. The presence of volunteers adds a richness and variety to the human resources of a museum to complement the specific nature of the collections from fine art treasures of national significance to everyday objects of local interest.

What has emerged from this study is not only the quality and quantity of volunteer activity in museums but also the importance of volunteer energy and enthusiasm in piloting new projects and in providing the means of support—financial and physical—for existing ones. What has become clear from the research is that volunteer involvement is integral to the ethos of all but the most specialist departmental university museums or private museums owned and run by individuals, and that volunteer support provides the essential under-pinning for the development of an expanding number of functions. In a majority of museums high public expectations and high professional standards cannot be met as far as the care of and access to collections are concerned without volunteer help.

The realisation by paid professional staff in museums that volunteers have a significant place within the museum community and are not a 'necessary nuisance' has created the climate whereby voluntary activity is no longer equated with amateurism. Volunteers and volunteer-led museums are no longer on the fringes of the museum movement. Nevertheless, the delineation of paid and unpaid posts and the definition of appropriate volunteer tasks remains an area of considerable sensitivity. Successful, well-managed volunteer pro-grammes distinguish clearly between the tasks undertaken by paid staff and those done by volunteers. Procedures and practices ensure that volunteers do not take over the jobs of paid staff. Conversely, volunteer activity often highlights the need for the creation of a paid position as part of the cycle of growth and development within an organisation.

A Changing Situation for Museums

Changes in the balance of the division of museums between the public sector, including National and Local Authority museums, and the Independent sector, including private museums and voluntary trusts, in favour of the independent sector and the introduction of the Museum Registration Scheme have brought issues concerning the management of volunteers to the fore. The recently established Museum Training Institute includes a major focus on volunteers as part of its remit to promote high standards of training within the museum profession. Changes and increases in the scope of the services provided by all museums in response to greater tourist, community and educational demand have reinforced the need for volunteers. Changes in the relationship between the government, local authorities and the voluntary sector have changed the role of voluntary organisations and given them an enhanced status. In these circumstances questions concerning policy planning and the management of volunteers are brought centre stage. This publication, *Volunteers in Museums and Heritage Organisations: Policy Planning and Management*, is designed to meet these new challenges.

2 | Setting the Agenda: The Volunteer Environment

The management of volunteers is an important aspect of the management of the multi-faceted resources of museums. Until recently, however, volunteers and volunteer-run museums were viewed as outsiders rather than integral to the museum community. They were the hidden face of museum professionalism. This is no longer the case. A positive attitude towards the partnership between volunteer and museum, combined with a sensitive insight into the reasons for the changing status of voluntary activity, are fundamental prerequisites for successful corporate planning and for establishing creative and effective management policies and practices.

The three sections below provide the context for management decisions in relation to the participation of volunteers. First, the growth of volunteer activity in museums is discussed both in terms of the emergence of the Voluntary Sector as a Third Sector—embracing those organisations that are neither public nor private—and an increased awareness of the community remit of museums. Second, the nature of current volunteer activity is explored in relation to differences in the size, purpose, management structures and management practices of museums in the United Kingdom. Third, different museum functions and areas of museum work are looked at in terms of issues concerning museum management and volunteer management. This sets the agenda for a detailed investigation into policy planning and policy implementation in subsequent chapters.

I: Volunteers as part of the Museum Community and part of the Wider Community.

The high profile of voluntary activity in the 1990s is the result of changing perceptions of the relationship between the state and society in general and the active participation of individuals within the community in particular. The principle of reciprocity inherent in voluntary activity engenders in people a sense of responsibility and ownership of their community. At the same time, it also offers them the opportunity for self-development and self-expression. The shift in the balance between statutory and voluntary bodies has been promoted by government policy and fresh insights into the inter-relationship between the formal and informal economies. This is enhanced by changing attitudes to work and current demographic trends. The social economy is no longer marginalised. It has moved from the twilight zone of the 'grey economy' to become significant in its own right.

There has been a convergence from opposite polarities to create the Third

5

Sector. This is illustrated clearly by recent developments within museums and heritage organisations. On the one hand, mutual support groups organised around enthusiasms or 'causes' such as local history museums or Railway Preservation Societies, once established, need to seek funds from outside sources to support their work. These may be charitable trusts, companies, government agencies such as the Museums and Galleries Commission, the Scottish Development Agency, the Highlands and Islands Development Board or the English Tourist Board, local authorities or European agencies such as the European Regional Development Fund. On the other hand, the notion of active citizenship—the free acceptance by individuals of voluntary obligations to the community of which they are members—is seen by the present government as a means of encouraging the personal responsibility of the individual to society. In addition, it is viewed as a means of renewing the social cohesion of a society that has been frayed during the last decades.[1]

Various incentives act as a spur for private and public companies to give financial contributions to voluntary bodies, second skilled staff and provide additional paid leave for staff spending time in voluntary service. The Association of Business Sponsorship of the Arts (ABSA) operates in an intermediary role for company giving to museums as well as to other arts organisations. The tradition of seconding teachers from local authorities to museums is well-established. Furthermore, Special employment measures like The Manpower Services Commission's Community Programme scheme, fostered the growth of the voluntary sector by providing 'paid' jobs. Only in exceptional cases has the Employment Training Programme, its successor, been able to meet the demands of museums and heritage organisations. The devastating effect of the impact of the loss in manpower to independent museums in particular with the demise of the Community Programme scheme emphasised the dangers of an over-reliance on short term expediency and the need for long term investment in human resources. The management of volunteers immediately gained importance.

The Voluntary Sector—Active Citizenship and Voluntary Activity

The principles and practice of active citizenship and voluntary activity combine to form the Voluntary or Third Sector. The dilemma identified by the Volunteer Centre UK is that active citizenship and voluntary activity are not synonymous. They are distinct but inter-connected activities. The quintessence of volunteering is the freedom of choice to 'take on something extra'. Voluntary activity 'transcends the political relationship between the state and its citizens'.[2] Voluntary activity, it is argued, has a separate value base from active citizenship. Overriding any such distinctions, however, it is important to recognise that the emergence of the voluntary sector as a whole as an acceptable field of service provision means a changing environment for volunteering in museums.

A measure of the novelty of the increased reliance on the voluntary sector by central and local government is that no official statistics exist. Precise figures for the number of voluntary bodies are not available. There were 160,000 registered Charities in 1988 but The National Council for Voluntary Organisations estimated in their evidence to the *Efficiency Scrutiny of Government Funding of the Voluntary Sector* that the total number of voluntary bodies was double this figure.[3] The sector has grown at the rate of 2% per annum since 1977. Some of this number includes museums and heritage organisations.

Parallel to the lack of statistical data on the voluntary sector as a whole, it is difficult to ascertain the exact proportion of museums organised on a voluntary basis within the Independent Sector. This heterogeneous amalgam represents approximately 1,250 museums—half the total number of museums in the United Kingdom—and is the sector in which the enormous expansion in the numbers of museums has taken place. Museums run by management committees of charitable trusts, local history groups, civic or amenity societies and preservation enthusiasts are not distinguished from those museums owned and run by private individuals or companies. A recent survey of the membership of the Association of Independent Museums carried out by the Policies Studies Institute and reported in *Cultural Trends 4 (1989)* revealed that volunteers outnumbered paid staff by 6 to 1 and that 23% of the respondents had no paid staff at all.[4]

Community Involvement

Community involvement, rather than simply the enthusiasm of volunteers, has been a major impetus in the rapid growth of museums over the past 25 years. Until now the significance of this has been undervalued and underestimated. What is required is a broadening in our understanding of the term community. Within the independent sector, small 'all-volunteer' local history museums have been placed in a separate category from the big industrial or transport museums with a core of paid professional staff.[5] In fact, both should be seen as part of a continuum of community participation in the recent phenomenal growth and development of museums under the umbrella of voluntary organisations. Museums as voluntary bodies have the autonomy and organisational flexibility to make a targeted response to new demands in a fast-changing world. Two thirds of all local history museums have opened since 1970 and 88% of current industrial museums were not in existence before that date.[6]

Communities of interest and community needs vary greatly. The Miles Report noted the increasing importance of the social uses of museums.[7] A community's search for its own identity and past roots often manifests itself through the creation of a museum. Such a search is itself, in part, a response to the accelerated rate of change in society. The tangible thread of continuity with the past represented by collections and expressed through exhibitions—either temporary or permanent—is indicative of a very special sense of belonging. The diversity in the interpretation of a common purpose is shown in the following examples. Ilchester is a one room museum established by incomers to this Somerset village, ostensibly as a means of improving village facilities. The former World War II air station nearby was the incentive to create an educational resource. Following almost three years of preparation and planning the museum is now open with a loaned collection, a rota of 20 volunteer stewards/helpers and a management sub-committee of four under the Town Trust.

Springburn Museum, Glasgow, is also a trust. It forms the focus of a community's fight back following the devastation and demoralisation caused by the closure of the British Rail works. The museum was set up with the explicit purpose of giving an historical perspective to the present and thereby helping the community to cope with change. Communal ownership is the philosophical base of the museum. A friendly atmosphere is a principal goal. Volunteers serve on the management committee and work in project teams in partnership with the paid curator and designer to plan and implement the policy of six temporary exhibitions a year. One centred on teenagers and addressed the 'generation gap' in Springburn. There are no permanent displays. Funding has been received from the Urban Programme and Glasgow District Council. Response to the immediate and specific needs of local communities in a state of flux, dictated by the tight constraints of a rural or urban setting within a small geographical area, are common characteristics of both museums. Interestingly, at Springburn the emphasis is on the impact of de-industrialisation rather than simply a celebration of the glories of Britain's industrial past.

This approach contrasts with the approach of most industrial and transport museums which have a single focus and a broad community base—a community of interest with a local, regional, national and, sometimes, an international remit. Beamish, North of England Open Air Museum, County Durham; the Weald and Downland Museum, Sussex and Ironbridge Gorge Museum, Shropshire are representative of the larger independent museums. The first is governed by a joint committee of the county, metropolitan borough and borough councils in the region and the second two are set up as charitable trusts. All aim to conserve the industrial past: all have paid staff including a Director. They charge for admission and compete as tourist attractions but their origins and continuing strength lie in close ties with the community. Both the Weald and Downland Museum and the National Tramway Museum, Crich, Derbyshire have residential accommodation for volunteers. (Case Study 4) Beamish still engages most of its active volunteers through the Friends organisation.

The development of Ironbridge Gorge Museum—now part of a UNESCO World Heritage Site—was dependent on the pioneering efforts of a dedicated group of volunteer trustees and other enthusiasts. As the self-proclaimed 'Birthplace of the Industrial Revolution' groups of Friends and fundraising supporters are located in Birmingham, London and the United States. The challenge for this particular independent museum in the 1990s is to balance the sometimes conflicting demands of different communities of interest. More tourists are needed to provide revenue. At the same time, they present problems in terms of the conservation of a unique environment and threaten the quality of life of the local community. The Iron Bridge is scheduled as an ancient monument; it belongs to the community of the nation. But the new Lady Wood bridge, planned to serve the needs of the local people living within the Gorge, would be within sight of a bridge of exceptional historic interest and international renown. Passion runs high and the problem was addressed in 1990 by a public enquiry.

Community involvement introduces the concept of a museum as a dynamic force in the process of change, orientated towards people as well as collections. The warmth of partisanship replaces the air of cool objectivity traditionally to be found in university, national and the larger local authority museums. Although this situation is changing too. In small local authority museums such as Peterborough (Case Study 6) civic pride and direct community involvement are more readily combined. In fact, many museums currently run by local authorities were started by volunteers.

The Formal and Informal Economy

A shift in the balance between statutory and voluntary bodies has already taken place within the museum sector. Therefore, a clear understanding of the relationship between the formal and informal economy is essential. Time rather than money is the means of exchange in the informal economy. Research by Jonathan Gershuny has shown that time is a measure of equivalent significance. We give time, we run out of time, we spend it, we are profligate, or mean with it, in just the same way as we are with money.[8] Yet, figures on the numbers of volunteers employed at individual museums and submitted in response to the survey carried out amongst members of the Association of Independent Museums by the Policy Studies Institute were often estimated. The report states: 'There is no indication of how many hours they work each week'.[9] The National Trust, on the other hand, is concerned with monitoring the cost effectiveness of volunteers. It ensures that the time given by volunteers is made meaningful within the framework of the formal economy by translating units of time into a monetary value. In the Mercia Region a total of 134,130 hours were worked in 1989 and rated at £410,200.

At the Smithsonian Institution, Washington DC, some 5,252 volunteers in the fiscal year 1989 provided services worth in excess of some $6 million. In the United States, however, the volunteer as well as the institution has a vested interest in recording the hours that s/he has contributed to the organisation. Tax relief is provided as an incentive for volunteering. In 1989, soon after the inauguration of the Bush administration, a television advertising campaign was mounted to encourage people to 'Give Five'—five per cent of their time or five per cent of their money to charitable organisations.

The Museum Registration Scheme

The Museum Registration Scheme implemented by the Museums and Galleries Commission acknowledges the interdependence of the formal and informal economy and gives public recognition to the changing relationship between statutory and voluntary bodies and the partnership between paid staff and volunteers. The scheme is a major factor in integrating volunteer-run museums and voluntary trusts within the museum community. It is a way of establishing minimum standards across the museum profession as a whole and, at the same time, gives recognition to the contribution made by volunteers. It is also a means of containing the further burgeoning of new museums of dubious quality.

Registration is voluntary, although non-registered museums are not eligible either for Museums and Galleries Commission or Area Museum Council funding, or subsidised curatorial and conservation services. Registration also provides a reference point for applications to other funding bodies. In order to register museums must comply with the definition of a museum adopted by the Museums Association in 1984 as '... an institution which collects, documents, preserves, exhibits and interprets material evidence and associated information for the public benefit'. Many of the museums seeking registration have been forced to ask themselves about the basis of their work. They are required to have an acceptable constitution, a firm financial underpinning and a collections management policy, have access to curatorial advice and provide a range of public services and facilities appropriate to the museum. Museums applying for registration are placed in one of five categories—full, provisional, deferred status, ineligible and rejection. There is an annual updating process and museums must reapply after 5 years. Museums run by volunteers can be assessed in the same way as museums in the public sector. This uniformity has raised the status and profile of independent museums.

There has been little opposition to the introduction of the Museum Registration Scheme. For the first time, critical help has been given to small, 'all-volunteer' museums which previously felt isolated. They have received advice and encouragement from the co-ordinating officers attached to the Area Museum Councils and direct support from County Museums Services. Many of these museums have plans for training programmes and skill development, including management training for trustees and honorary officers. Cheshire Museums Services Unit (CMSU) has a large number of 'all-volunteer' museums. A curatorial advisor who works in close association with the North West Museums Services (NWMS) is helping these museums to carry out registration procedures. The Museum of South Somerset receives curatorial advice from the County Museums Officer and shares a documentation assistant with other museums. It is launching a programme of basic conservation with advice from the County Museum Conservation Officer. A post for a paid curator has recently been approved. Other areas are not so lucky. In Dorset, for example, where there are over 35 'all-volunteer' museums, there is no County Museum Service although one is planned for 1991.

One of the principal advantages of registration is that it shows up the weaknesses within an organisation. Most museums have had to produce new acquisitions and collections management policies. Crewkerne Museum has drawn up an acquisitions policy in order to meet registration requirements. Conservation and documentation are major areas of concern. Some of the larger independent museums have been put in the position of reviewing policies on the care of collections. Ironbridge Gorge Museum now has a Collections Manager.

One special interest group that is presented with particular problems by the Museum Registration Scheme is the Association of Railway Preservation Societies. As a result of a working party set up in 1989 to examine how these societies would fit into the scheme help has been given to improve documentation and cataloguing. The major issue, however, is that virtually every railway has a unique collection of locomotives, rolling stock, stations etc. that it restores and uses, thus challenging the central museum concept that objects should be collected for posterity. The constitutions of many societies add to the problem. Some societies, however, do have 'museums' on their sites. A railway must now determine precisely what is in its collection and distinguish between what will be used in the present and what will be preserved for future generations.

The Contract Culture

A further development may either enhance or diminish the status of a number of voluntary sector museums, especially those with substantial grant-in-aid from local authorities. The impact on museums of the 'Contract Culture' and the rapid growth in service delivery by voluntary organisations as a result is, as yet unknown. The contracting out of services by local authorities through Compulsory Competitive Tendering is at an early stage of development. The provision of a Museum Service by local authorities, however, is discretionary and not mandatory.[10] Some authorities have already shifted provision from the basis of direct funding to core funding by establishing charitable trusts. Torfaen Museum Trust, Pontypool and Pallant House, Chichester are examples. What is certain is that those museums providing a bad service and those representing poor value for money may well be under threat. Museum Registration is important here; so too, is the specification drawn up by the museum. The Museums and Galleries Commission is currently undertaking research into Local Authorities and Museums and the Audit Commission has terms of reference for an enquiry into *Local Authority Support for Museums, the Arts, Cultural Activities and Entertainment*. In a climate of accountability the need for museums run by volunteers or voluntary trusts to scrutinise, identify and evaluate the various aspects of their activities in terms of the cost-effectiveness and value of the service provision to the community may become increasingly important. The Local Government and Housing Act (1989) has already made it less easy for charitable trusts to set up subsidiary companies.

II: Volunteer Activity—Management Structures and Management Practices

The commitment, inspiration and dedication of volunteers, however, is not only channelled into setting up, managing and working in voluntary organisations within the independent sector; it is also an important source of support for museums in the public sector—National, Local Authority and University museums. Boards of Trustees, Associations of Friends, supporters clubs and NADFAS Volunteers provide an outer network of patronage within the community and practical help within the organisation. Other volunteers give direct assistance to paid staff.

Formal acknowledgement of the contribution of volunteers to museums in the public sector is, in part, an acceptance of the new status of voluntary activity, and in part pragmatic. Volunteers have always worked behind the scenes. Findings from the Museums' Database, reported in *Museums UK* (1987), revealed that in 40% of National, Local Authority and Independent Museums volunteers undertake the important job of information processing relating to collections— responsible for documentation, library work and research[11]. The results further indicate that volunteers are used more extensively for interpretive functions such as guiding in the independent sector than in the public sector. Yet, until recently, the work of volunteers was often unappreciated. One person commented to Jenny Mattingly during her survey on *Volunteers in Museums and Galleries* (1984): 'Volunteers are to be seen and not heard or given credit'.[12] This situation is changing. A diversity of functions is now expected of public sector museums to meet the multiplicity of demands and high expectations of tourists, students and members of the community. The need to provide greater access to collections and, simultaneously, the need to maintain high standards of collections management without a significant increase in direct funding means that a dismissive approach to volunteers is no longer appropriate or possible. Volunteers are needed: they are a valuable resource.

Recognition of the volunteer contribution as part of the assets of a museum has highlighted the need for museums in the public sector to consider the organisation of volunteers within the museum management structure. Two main changes are taking place. First, staff are being appointed to supervise projects involving volunteers and second, the role of Friends Associations is being reviewed.

Volunteer Organisers

Following the lead of a number of the larger independent museums such as Beamish, Ironbridge and, more recently, the Museum of Science and Industry in Manchester (Case Study 3) publicly-funded bodies are starting to appoint Volunteer Co-ordinators or to give staff responsibility for the supervision of volunteers as part of their job description. The Victoria and Albert Museum, for example, has a member of the Education Department in charge of the newly-created programme of volunteer guides. Part of the job of one of the members of the Marketing Department is to liaise with the Friends who run the Information Desk. (Case Study 1) The Ashmolean Museum operates an Education Service on an autonomous basis through volunteer assistance. It is led by the unpaid Volunteer Co-ordinator whose energy and enthusiasm established the service almost nine years ago. Glasgow Museum and Art Gallery's Guiding Service was set up at the same time and operates in four of its nine museums. The guides are organised through the Friends, the Glasgow Art Gallery and Museums Association, and it, too, has a 'volunteer' co-ordinator who is responsible for over one hundred and seventy guides. At The Merseyside Maritime Museum, part of the National Museums and Galleries on Merseyside but formerly under local authority control, the unpaid co-ordinator looks after over two hundred 'active' volunteers and works in conjunction with a liaison post on the staff.

In many smaller local authority museums such as Horsham Museum, Surrey, where volunteers are encouraged as a matter of policy, the responsibility for organising the rota of some thirty to forty people who volunteer to work in the shop or on the information desk, as well as arranging specific tasks to suit the skills of individual volunteers, is part of the curator's job. A retired solicitor is cataloguing legal documents. One local volunteer works at The British Museum on the computerisation of the documents collection but carries out his special interest hobby at Horsham Museum and is restoring a model.

Friends Associations

Friends organisations are traditionally identified with a supportive fund-raising role. But many Friends Associations offer far more to their museums than a supporters group and a platform for fund-raising and appeals, although these two functions remain important. The question is often asked 'What is the difference between a Friend and a volunteer?' The answer is not straightforward. 'Active' Friends are generally classified as those people who are part of a Friends organisation who give 'hands on' help within the organisation, for example, as financial advisers, guides, shop assistants and wardens, or by contributing to conservation and curatorial work. The definition is misleading in the sense that attending fund-raising committees and organising auctions or appeals is 'active' involvement and commitment to the museum or gallery. Moreover, an individual may be a 'sleeping volunteer', accruing the benefits from membership and attending social gatherings, until retirement when s/he is able to offer practical help.

Three categories of Friends are identifiable in museums; first, there are members who pay a subscription and occasionally attend social events; second, there are Friends who are active supporters in that they participate in fund-raising activities and third, there are Friends who give active help in a 'hands-on' capacity. At Beamish Museum, the latter group are called 'Friends volunteer workers'. In this publication the term 'active' Friend is used to describe hands-on help because this is the one used by curators and managers who work with Friends and Supporters Groups which straddle the divide between offering externally orientated fund-raising and public relations activities on the one hand and practical assistance on a regular basis within the museum on the other. At the Merseyside Maritime Museum, Friends fulfil a fund-raising and public relations role and operate volunteer teams including a Boat Maintenance Team that logged 4,000 hours of work in 1984. Incentives are provided in the form of star ratings. They also act as the 'pioneer corps' and test new ideas: at present these include a play boat for children.[13]

The recruitment of volunteers through Friends organisations is important in the independent sector because an Association can provide insurance cover. In both the independent and the public sectors, in certain instances, there is split responsibility for the recruitment of volunteers. Some volunteer help is organised directly by individual curators or keepers and some is organised through Friends Associations. Beamish and Birmingham City Museum and Art Gallery are examples. Such fragmentation can add to the difficulties in maintaining standardised management practices.

The potential of Friends to give assistance in a targeted rather than in a generalised manner is the subject of a major review by Birmingham Museum and Art Gallery. In a cost-benefit analysis, the extent and availability of the skills of Friends is being examined alongside the effectiveness of the Friends organisation in terms of public relations and in gaining sponsorship through local contacts. Once these vast resources are utilised, as they are at Merseyside Maritime Museum and The Whitworth Art Gallery Manchester. (Case Study 2) Friends organisations can no longer be viewed as satellites but as having a particular role, or a number of roles, within the management structure of the museum as a whole.

The Partnership—Volunteers and Paid Staff

The nature of the partnership between volunteers and paid staff will vary according to the size and type of management structure in the organisation and differences in the nature and value of the collections. These two factors affect both the range of museum functions undertaken by volunteers and the degree of responsibility they have within each. The pattern of volunteer involvement in key museum functions is compared across a sample of National, Local Authority and Independent museums in Appendix I. Guiding in all types of museums is provided by volunteers. Security, on the whole, is handled by paid staff with the exception of some open air museums and 'all-volunteer' local history collections. This is in line with advice from the National Museums Security Adviser who considers that the attendant's job is too important to be left to volunteers although he recognises they are being used.[14] It should be borne in mind that there is a marked contrast between, for example, the sale-room value of a painting in the National Gallery and farm tools at The Weald and Downland Museum.

A major difference is identifiable in the role of volunteers in Information Services in some of the larger publicly funded museums and the larger independent museums. This hinges on the definition of 'core' functions. Traditionally 'core' functions relate simply to the care of collections. Increasingly, however, 'core' functions include the care of visitors as well. At the Victoria and Albert Museum and the National Maritime Museum—national museums receiving grant-in-aid—the Information Desks are run by Friends and viewed as support activities. Whereas, at the Museum of Science and Industry in Manchester and Ironbridge Gorge Museum—independent museums dependent to a large extent on revenue income from ticket sales—visitor reception is seen as a 'core' activity of primary importance. This situation may change as a consequence of the introduction of entrance charges. At present, a parallel can be found in the United States where The Smithsonian Institution—a national museum—is free and volunteers operate the Information Desks. At the Boston Museum of Science—an independent nonprofit organisation—where an entrance fee is charged, paid personnel run the visitor reception facilities.

Volunteers not only undertake different functions in different museums, but their experiences in the same area of work can be very different according to the type of the organisation in which they are working. Volunteers who work for the Archive Section of the Tate Gallery—a national institution—and those who work for Whitby Pictorial Archives Trust—staffed almost entirely by volunteers with a small number of Employment Training places—are operating in the same museum resource area. At the Tate Gallery projects require a high level of accuracy and tasks such as sorting and filing exhibition catalogues can be somewhat monotonous. At Whitby Archives, however, the work for project teams is far more wide ranging. It includes pictorial research, the maintenance of an oral history archive and dealing with enquiries into family history as well as filing and documentation.

Whether paid staff or volunteers lead a project can make a critical difference. The *Policy Statement on Volunteers* produced by the Museums Association 'Acknowledges the important part which voluntary helpers and members of the Museum Societies can play in Museums and Art Galleries in supplementing and supporting the permanent professional staff of a museum'. Significantly, the statement stresses the support role of volunteers to a core of paid staff—one echoed in the Policy Planning and Procedures at the Museum of Science and Industry in Manchester (Case Study 3)—but it neither takes account of voluntary trusts where management committees act in an executive capacity, nor does it satisfactorily address the situation where Friends and/or volunteers outnumber paid staff and are responsible for organising projects or events with the assistance of paid advisers rather than vice versa. A comparison between the Education Services offered by Somerset Museum of Rural Life, Glastonbury—a local authority museum—and Dulwich Picture Gallery—a private foundation—offers real contrasts. At the former, the peripatetic County Museum Education Officer visits the museum to work alongside Friends to research and develop special educational activities for schools. At the latter, the site-based Education Officer works with a small group of highly-qualified, highly-trained volunteers who are all ex-teachers. Different services are provided. Whilst at one, there is focus on thematic work, at the other, there are no standardised visits.

Volunteer expert advisers have a special relationship with the Museum Director and senior management. Their knowledge, understanding and influence can be extremely valuable even though their time commitment is limited. At The Science Museum an Engineering Committee meets every four months. Other committees advise on collections policy and the availability of acquisitions in the fields of plastics, printing and space. In return they are given a good lunch and the opportunity to make effective use of their expertise for the benefit of posterity. Whatever the differences between the nature of the relationship between paid staff and volunteers which will determine, to some extent, the nature of the work done by each, the principle of reciprocity remains the same.

Policies, Practices and Procedures

Similarly, 'good practice', in managing volunteer involvement or the self-management of volunteers crosses the boundaries of the public and private sectors as well as different organisational structures. It is important, therefore, to review current management practices and procedures in museums.

With notable exceptions, it appears that management practices are falling behind the growth of volunteer involvement in museums and galleries. Examples of good practice are outlined in Appendix II. In general, museums take an unsophisticated, laissez-faire attitude to the management of volunteers. Procedures are frequently piecemeal and ad hoc rather than explicit and formalised. However, they provide the foundation for the development of standardised practices. Where brief statements do exist they are designed primarily to protect the interests of the volunteer and the museum authorities. They come in different guises, labelled variously 'Arrangements for Volunteers' (Catalyst, Museum of the Chemical Industry), 'Conservation Interns in the Department of Conservation' (National Maritime Museum), and 'Draft Volunteer Agreement' (Merseyside Museums). What is clear is that there is some confusion about what constitutes a volunteer policy, guidelines, a volunteer agreement and, in some cases, a code of practice.

'Guidelines for the Engagement of Voluntary Assistants' prepared by the National Museums of Scotland in 1986 have been accepted by the management and trade union side. Agreement has been reached that volunteers will not undertake 'basic operational work'. Details of policy, acceptance procedures and general conditions of work are included, but the guidelines do not relate to student placements. The 'Volunteer Policy' drawn up by the Yorkshire and Humberside Museums Council, however, is designed to cover students. It includes graduates wanting to undertake work experience as a prerequisite for admission on to a postgraduate course in museum studies and undergraduate students taking museum/art and design courses. It is similar in content to the guidelines from the National Museums of Scotland.

Many large local authority and national museums take a low key approach. This is shown by the 'Arrangements for Volunteers' in the Costume Department at the Museum of London: 'From time to time, as museum commitments allow, volunteers and students are taken on to help in the Costume Department .... Volunteers and students work alongside the curatorial staff on whatever work is currently taking place in the Department'. No structured programme exists; volunteers are not paid fees or expenses. They are not usually allowed to undertake research and they are not employed to take part in conservation work. Their work is very restricted.

Many independent and small local authority museums take a contrasting approach. At Beamish Museum, Co. Durham, 'Friends Volunteer Workers' are high profile. The tone of the documentation is different and the range of tasks are many and varied. They include site clearance, talks and lectures, administration, restoration and maintenance, demonstrating, acting as car park attendants and occasional research. The Notes begin 'What do Friends do?' and continue 'A large part of the work we do is suited to active people who don't mind getting dirty and a certain amount of it is in the open air'. They stress the need to accept the aims and objectives of the Friends of Beamish Museum, team work, being flexible, being reliable, being enthusiastic and being prepared for training. A separate Safety Policy has a separate section on volunteers. Peterborough Museum has a 'Contract for Volunteers' that begins "Welcome to Peterborough Museum. We are grateful to you for offering us your services and we look forward to having you working with us". The contract also includes guidelines. (Case Study 6)

Dunwich Museum is an example a small volunteer-run museum. Here there is a conflation between volunteer policy and management policy and practice. Museum officers, including the Hon. Curator, are appointed from 'the general body of trustees' to operate the museum day to day. Prominent acknowledgement of the limitations of local volunteer input and the importance of membership of the Association for Suffolk Museums and reliance on paid professional help is included in the documentation. 'While the museum will make all reasonable use of the service of volunteers, especially from the village and its neighbourhood, for the running of the museum, the trustees should also ensure access to professional support services which a small museum can not expect to find from its own resources'.

Training

Training provision for volunteers is at a more advanced stage of development. The Area Museum Councils offers a range of training courses and the South West Area Museums Service has recently organised a course on basic preventive conservation techniques. The training of volunteers is one of three principal objectives of the newly formed Museum Training Institute. Training can revitalize a flagging service. This has been the experience of the Sainsbury Centre for Visual Arts at the University of East Anglia. Ten years after the Centre was opened there were a dwindling number of guides. Then a rigorous training programme was introduced by the Deputy Keeper amidst considerable consternation and there is now a waiting list. The introduction of a structured training scheme has helped rather than hindered recruitment and, at the same time, has integrated the Friends guiding scheme into the management structure of the Centre.

III: Museum Management and Volunteer Management

Museums have specific concerns in relation to the management of volunteers and these issues need to be addressed. Three aspects of museum work are singled out for discussion—curatorship, conservation and education. Before this, however, the term professional requires careful definition.

Profession and a Professional Approach

In the strictest sense, argues Kenneth Hudson, working in museums is not a profession since a traditional profession—doctor or lawyer—is made up of an association of independent people who are licensed to practice. He also notes that 'professional' is a vague catch-all and 'appears to mean little more than 'full-time', 'paid' or 'highly-skilled'.[15] The Museum Registration Scheme rewards the skill and competence of museum staff whether or not they have passed the Museums Association Diploma, or have degrees in Conservation, or whether they are paid or unpaid. The Museums and Galleries Commission do, however, recommend the use of expert advice. Clear distinctions need to be made. The Cookworthy Museum was able to make effective use of volunteers only through the expert advice, planning and policies of a consultant curator. (Case Study 5) A management review of a leading local authority museum revealed that, even in a big public institution, curators, by and large, see themselves as independent experts rather than managers or co-ordinators of teams of staff.

In this publication a professional approach is used to cover both volunteers and paid staff. The criteria are skill and competence; reliability and accountability and an ability to achieve goals. The word expert is reserved for those who have training, qualifications and/or a life-time or experience in a specific area of museum work. 'A professional staff demands professional volunteers' stated Barbara Kelly, Denver Art Museum, in 1986.[16] The visitor makes no distinction between a volunteer or paid staff. Both represent the museum and are responsible for its 'professional' image. This does not mean the replacement of warmth and friendliness by a clinical coldness. A professional approach means that all those working for the museum feel part of the organisation and know what it aims to achieve. They are confident as well as competent in their relations with the general public; welcoming as well as efficient. From the point of view of paid staff, a clear volunteer policy and procedures are essential in order that volunteers have openly acknowledged parameters within which to operate. (Case Studies 8b,c) Working relations suffer when the boundaries are blurred.

Curatorship

Curatorship as a concept is, in many ways, out of date. It is no longer possible for one person to be omni-competent. The number of functions expected to be undertaken by curators has grown and each one has its own technical know-how and complexities. Curators have become managers. A plethora of Hon. Curators in charge of small local history museums, like departmental curators and keepers in larger museums, are increasingly required to bring in specialists for research, documentation, design, conservation, marketing and development purposes. The Museums and Galleries Commission, Area Museums Councils, Museum Documentation Association and private consultants provide advice and support. Research for this project indicates that in smaller museums, traditional curatorial tasks such as documentation, research and exhibition work are done increasingly by volunteers since curators are required to use their expertise in managerial roles.

In this shift to the position of curator/manager it is important that good collections management is balanced with good human resource management. A recognisable change has taken place in the pattern of working relations within organisations in the late twentieth century. Charles Handy discusses these developments in *The Future of Work* (1985) and, more recently, in the *Age of Unreason* (1989).[17] A 'core' paid staff is supported by paid experts, on the one hand, and volunteers on the other. This has always been the situation in the independent sector, but it is becoming increasingly common in the public sector. Where the dividing line is drawn between tasks for paid staff, outside experts and volunteers can only be decided by curators/managers on the basis of the priorities of individual museums. At Peterborough and Springburn Museums lively exhibition programmes would not be possible without volunteer help and support. Peterborough also uses volunteers to help with documentation: Springburn uses paid experts for conservation.

Conservation

Conservation can be a contentious area as far as volunteers are concerned. Low standards can cause irreparable damage to artefacts and put collections at risk. Conservation is a new specialism within museums and conservators themselves are often 'made to feel subsidiary to the need of curators,' according to the *UKIC Survey: Conservation Facilities in Museums and Galleries* (1989).[18] This situation is compounded by the increasing volume of work and the widespread use of volunteers—33% in National, 30% in Local Authority and 48% in the Independent Museums, where supervision is least tight.

The supervision of volunteers undertaking conservation work is the key issue. The 'unfettered use of volunteers' is identified as a major problem by the Head of the Conservation Unit at the Museum and Galleries Commission. The reluctance of paid conservators to supervise volunteers is seen as the main obstacle to their use except in museums run by volunteers in the report on

The Conservation of Industrial Collections (1989).[19] Supervision is time-consuming: but it is less a question of individual sensibilities and more one of the well-being of the objects. A high level of experience and judgement is required when dealing with antiquities and works of art, many of which require individual assessment of their condition and continuous monitoring of treatment as it progresses. Awareness training is needed. What is important is that curators/managers—paid and unpaid alike—should be able to recognise when a specialist conservator is required. They should be trained to understand that unsupervised conservation or restoration by volunteers is inappropriate 'except with adequate training on agreed tasks' as the Scottish Museums Council's *Conservation Survey of Museum Collections* (1989) pointed out.[20]

The answer to the question 'What conservation tasks can volunteers do?' will depend on the approach and resources of individual museums. In national museums, conservation internships provide professional training and support for paid staff. At the opposite end of the spectrum, the all-volunteer conservation team at Ruddington Museum do all but the most specialist tasks under supervision following training. (Case Study 7) At Cheltenham Museum and Art Gallery, a local authority museum, the scope for volunteers is strictly limited. For security reasons they are not allowed to handle objects although two seamstresses help with the costume collection and others clean metalwork. At Quarry Bank Mill, Styal, Cheshire a carefully selected group of students worked under supervision to transfer a collection to a new site. They carried out documentation, packing, labelling and basic conservation measures after first receiving training. In fact, a great deal of the conservation work currently undertaken by volunteers is in the field of preventive conservation—the area highlighted for immediate attention by the Scottish Museums Council's report. This includes environmental monitoring and control; for example, checking levels of relative humidity and temperature, visible light, ultraviolet radiation and particulate pollution.

NADFAS Volunteers make a major contribution in the area of preventive conservation. Their formalised procedures, training methods and approach to working with paid staff are exemplary. (Appendix III) A code of conduct has been agreed between NADFAS, The Historic Houses Association and The Museums Association. This responds to the need to define terms and ensure that the correct training and supervision of work are provided, especially in areas like the conservation of textiles and book refurbishment. Library work is a major feature of the work of NADFAS Volunteers. They have contributed to schemes at the Advocates Library under the supervision of the Chief Book Conservator for the National Library of Scotland. At the Horniman Museum their assistance in preparing objects for exhibition or storage under the instruction of paid conservators—cleaning, repairing, measuring, labelling and repacking a variety of materials like bones, bark, cloth, basketry, metal, pottery and wood—has released paid staff to undertake more specialist tasks. The few hours trained staff do spend with groups on a regular weekly basis is more than repaid by their work.

The tradition of volunteer enthusiasts undertaking the majority of conservation work at industrial and transport museums is changing. Neglect of collections is causing concern. But there are examples of volunteer restoration schemes meeting the highest standards, including Kew Bridge Steam Engines and the 80 horsepower Fielding Engine restored by members of the mid-Gloucester Engine Preservation Society at The National Waterways Museum which won the Dorothea Award in 1988. Finding trained conservators in this field is difficult and has prompted the introduction of an in-service training course for technicians by The Science Museum. In addition, a conservation workshop has been established at Wroughton airfield. Trained technicians work with specially selected volunteers and check standards. Training is also given in the ethics of conservation: the need to avoid the unlimited destruction of original surfaces and to record machinery before it is dismantled is pointed out. Mutual respect and understanding is of paramount importance in this scheme since a trained, volunteer engineer may be instructed by a trained, paid conservator who is not an engineer. In the field of conservation, as in other areas of museum work, experts in other disciplines who volunteer to work in museums need to be trained to adapt their expertise to the specific requirements of the museum profession.

Education

The legacy of a tremendous growth in the numbers of museums in the independent sector and a focus on exhibitions and displays in museums in the public sector in the 1980s affected education as much as conservation. Museum education reached a plateau. In many instances the gap in provision for leisure learning and formal learning requirements has been provided by volunteer guides, often organised by Friends Associations. With the maturing of many 'new' museums and a re-assessment of the importance of access to collections, the status of guiding is changing from being considered a low level task to one of critical importance to the public profile of museums.

At the development stage new museums such as the Mary Rose Trust, Portsmouth, and the Merseyside Maritime Museum, Liverpool, needed volunteer guides to show people what was happening both to satisfy public curiosity following wide-scale media coverage and to ensure the safety of visitors. Now, Friends at the Merseyside Maritime Museum offer a 'slide-guide' service to pre-booked parties. The Guide Leader maintains standards through a written and oral test for new guides following a series of lectures. Friends run the guide services at Birmingham and Glasgow City Museums and Art Galleries. A survey on 'Friends as Volunteer Guides in Museums' carried out by the Sainsbury Centre for Visual Arts at the University of East Anglia and reported in the BAFM Yearbook, 1989–90, notes 'the great diversity in size, content and organisation of the services offered to the public'.[21] It stresses the need for guiding services that operate through Friends Associations to have adequate representation within the organisation and the need for training to ensure respect for the boundaries between paid staff and volunteers. Formal procedures avert potential sources of friction. Guide training schemes, for example at the Tate Gallery in London, have been modelled largely on the docent (guide) programmes in American museums. (Case Study 8) In the United States and in Italy there is a major focus on educational guiding for schools and this has been an important growth area in the United Kingdom in recent years.

At the Tate Gallery, guides support the work of the Education Department. They provide special lectures for young children and help to develop interaction with older children by taking the role of 'guide animatrice'. Through ACE

(Action for Children's Education) groups they assist with the acclimatisation of families and children unfamiliar with art galleries. The Ashmolean Museum, Oxford, provides a guiding service tailored to the needs of individual schools. At the Natural History Museum, London, fifty 'auxiliaries'—mainly retired school teachers—undertake a programme of training and evaluation over 3–4 years. They give conducted tours to pupils of primary school age and advise secondary teachers on available resources. The Education Officer at the Chiltern Open Air Museum is assisted by volunteer guides, many of whom are also retired school teachers. The highlight of a two hour tour is lighting a fire in the Iron Age House. Tours at Quarry Bank Mill last one and a half hours. Volunteers trained by Education staff offer a series of thematic options: red—how the factory system began; blue—what it was like to live and work at Styal; orange—textiles today.

Consideration needs to be given as to whether the educational needs of school children are best served through the use of volunteers giving guided tours. The emphasis in the National Curriculum is on investigative learning and problem solving by children through first-hand experience. Even 'dialogue,' to use an American phrase, does not satisfy the need to hand over the enquiry to the pupils since discussion is 'directed' by the guide. There is, however, an increasing role for volunteers as facilitators and resources for learning. Exhibit demonstrators at Blists Hill Site, Ironbridge Gorge Museum, answer questions as they show children how the machinery worked in the candle factory or what it was like to live in a squatter's cottage. Nothing can surpass the voluntary Education Officer at the Manchester Jewish Museum recounting his experiences as a child in a prison camp in Dachau. This is a resource and first-hand experience of a very special kind.

The high quality of Education Services in smaller museums is frequently the result of the creative use of volunteers within programme planning. At Dulwich trained volunteers meet the requirements of individual schools. At Somerset Museum of Rural Life the volunteer contribution allows investigative learning sessions to take place, including the handling of selected objects; at Godalming Museum an experimental Education Service was started in 1989. Led by the Museum Assistant, volunteers prepared a 'Wool Pack'—including artefacts and leaflets—for loan to schools. Sessions held at Guildford Teachers Centre explained Godalming's links with the wool and knitting industries and gave teachers the opportunity to explore how they could use this in thematic, cross-curricular and subject based work. Through outreach programmes, by providing intensive supervision and by acting as facilitators, or oral history resources in their own right, volunteers can give breadth and depth to museum education.

Volunteers

Volunteering in museums has developed separately from other forms of volunteering. People who are attracted to volunteer in museums, galleries and at historic sites are motivated primarily from a commitment to the resource within the community rather than a commitment to the plight of people within the community. The chance to meet like-minded people, stave off loneliness, use their expertise or add to their own knowledge in a life-long education are some of the other factors that motivate people to volunteer to work in museums. Each has a personal agenda. Among the many different volunteers in museums, some require particular mention.

Disabled People

Access for disabled people to museums is far more than providing ramps and wheelchairs, although these are essential. *Arts for Everyone* (1985) provides guidance on facilities for disabled people and discusses such issues as 'touch' exhibits and induction loops.[22] Where volunteers can help most is that they have time to give to people and time to talk. They are available in sufficient numbers to provide one-to-one contact when necessary. At the Victoria and Albert Museum there are guided tours for the visually impaired and at the Whitworth Art Gallery an outreach and visits programme is designed to meet the needs of disabled, elderly, infirm and visually handicapped residents of retirement homes, day centres and occupational therapy departments in hospitals. VAMI guides have prepared a braille plan for Milan Cathedral. (Appendix III)

In an imaginative project at the Smith Art Gallery, Stirling during 1988, volunteers worked with paid staff and groups of mentally handicapped children and adults to create an environment in the main hall called 'Sons and Daughters of the Rock.' Through a mixture of drama, music, song and dance 272 handicapped people explored life in the city in 1788 and finally came together in a procession, waving flags, singing marching songs and taking part in a celebratory ceilidh.

Disabled people also present an untapped pool of potential volunteers. This issue and the recruitment of other special constituencies including ethnic minorities is discussed in Chapter 4.

Student Volunteers

Student volunteer involvement in museums and galleries in work experience schemes, student placements and internships as part of a course of study or in preparation for a paid professional career in museums raises different issues. A period of voluntary service as a prerequisite for entry into the museum profession was criticised in the Hale Report on *Museum Professional Training and Career Structure* on the grounds that, amongst other reasons, it can favour the 'well off' and contributes to the amateur reputation of the museum profession.[23] This publication takes a broader view. A professional approach is considered important for all volunteers working in museums, including student volunteers.

What is at issue here is that museum staff give administrative and supervision time in arranging projects and training students out of good will on an ad hoc basis. This system can be mutually advantageous and individual relationships established between colleges, students and museum staff are generally excellent. They are idiosyncratic rather than bureaucratic. Nevertheless, the lack of student bursaries, lack of guidelines and lack of co-ordination of training as it currently exists means that there is an increasing demand for short placements of between 2–4 weeks. This is an added burden for generous-spirited museum staff without the two way benefit of an extended attachment of between 2–6 months.

A Working Party of The Association of Art Historians has examined the question of student volunteers and made the following recommendations:-

- That sole responsibility for volunteer placements within higher education cannot be left to individual museums and institutions acting ad hoc.

- That guidelines for museums, students, etc. possibly with standard application and monitoring procedures should be developed as part of The Museum Training Institute's programme.

- That there should be a nationally advertised programme of training based in participating organisations under the aegis of The Museum Training Institute. A system of grant aid or bursaries should be considered.

Retired People

There are large numbers of retired people working in museums. This is atypical compared to the national picture of volunteering generally. The Vale and Downland Museum arranges short shifts to accommodate them. Enthusiasts—mainly men—form another group who provide practical help at industrial and transport museums at weekends and in their holidays. The fear here is that they are an aging constituency and their skills and time may not be replaced by a new generation. (Case Study 4)

Women Volunteers

Guiding is undertaken principally by women in both the United Kingdom and in the United States. (Case Studies 1 and 8) The stereotyped museum volunteer as a 'middle-aged woman who has raised her family and now wants to do something useful for the community and for herself' is not entirely inaccurate.[24] Members of the Ladies Committee of The Boston Museum of Fine Art provide flower arrangements, cookies and cakes for afternoon tea and a rota for the Information Desk in addition to Guided Tours. They are invited to belong. The Boston Museum of Science attracts none of this group of long term volunteers and offers ingenious short term opportunities for those in work. (Case Study 9)

National Volunteer Organisations

The development of national organisations of volunteers world-wide reflects the changing position of volunteers within museums. These include The British Association of Friends of Museums (BAFM), the National Association of Decorative and Fine Art Societies (NADFAS) Volunteers (NVs), the Voluntari Associati Per I Musei Italiani (VAMI) and the American Association of Museum Volunteers (AAMV). (Appendix III) The need for a central body to define policy and co-ordinate the activities of dispersed groups with a common aim is part of the move towards increased professionalism, greater specialisation and recognition by the museum community as a whole that volunteers and paid staff must work in partnership.

The value of volunteer organisations to museums cannot be underestimated. Not only do they raise the standards and expectations of volunteers through newsletters, publications and the introduction of procedures but they also create a network of volunteer supporters of museums that operate at local, regional, national and international levels. There is a World Federation of Friends of Museums (WFFM). The advantages are two-fold: volunteers have a voice in a variety of public arenas and government departments and associations of museum professionals know who to consult on questions of volunteer involvement.

Underlying the commitment of these organisations to improve the quality, quantity and status of volunteering is the commitment to provide members with a forum for social interchange and 'educational enrichment'. Thus, programmes of talks are combined with programmes of concerts and fund-raising parties. Social cohesion is of immense value in rooting a museum in the community in which it is located. This is true just as much for national museums as for small local history collections.

Volunteers in the Future

There will be great competition for staff by organisations, including museums, in the 1990s. Women—a traditional pool of volunteer labour in museums—can no longer be relied on as a steady source of supply. Different patterns of work mean that men and women who choose to be self-employed, or to undertake part-time work may also choose to volunteer. By far the largest source of potential volunteers, however, are those in the age group 50–70, many of whom have taken early retirement. *Social Trends* (1990) noted that in 1988 retired men had most leisure time.[25] This group already contributes to supporting museum activities. In addition, museums have the opportunity to recruit volunteers from groups that are currently under-represented. These include members of the black community and those with disabilities.

What is needed to attract volunteers in increasing numbers to museums and heritage organisations in the 1990s is clear policy planning and the introduction of procedures and practices designed specifically to meet the needs of volunteers. This does not mean introducing a system of rewards or, indeed, the stress of paid work, but the opportunities and satisfactions associated with that framework. It will require an open recruitment policy, a regular timetable, a clearly defined task and role within the organisation, a well publicised but unobtrusive system for the payment of out-of-pocket expenses and the chance to contribute expertise and make social contacts. By taking the best from both the formal and informal economies, managers of volunteers in museums and self-managed all-volunteer museums have a firm foundation for recruiting, keeping and using volunteers effectively. This will serve to support and sustain the growth and development of museums and heritage organisations into the twenty-first century.

Notes

[1] Hurd, Douglas, 'Freedom will Flourish where Citizens accept Responsibility', *The Independent*, 13/09/89.

[2] Willis, Elaine, Foreword to *Active Citizenship: Myth or Reality?* The Volunteer Centre UK, 1989, p.1.

[3] Home Office, *Efficiency Scrutiny of Government Funding in the Voluntary Sector. Profiting from Partnership*, HMSO, 1990.

[4] Feist, Andrew and Hutchison, Robert, *Cultural Trends 4*, Policy Studies Institute, December 1989.

[5] Cossons, Neil, Article on Volunteers in Thompson, J. Aird (ed) *Manual of Curatorship. A Guide to Museum Practice*, Butterworths, 1984, p.86.

[6] *Cultural Trends 4*, p.19.

[7] Museums and Galleries Commission *Museums in Scotland: Report by a Working Party*, HMSO, 1986.

[8] Gershuny, Jonathan, *Social Innovation and Division of Labour*, Oxford University Press, 1983.

[9] *Cultural Trends 4*, p.22.

[10] *Public Libraries and Museums Act*, 1964, Sections 12–15.

[11] Prince, David and Higgins-McLoughlin, Bernadette, *Museum UK*, Museums Association, 1987, pp.98 and 104.

[12] Mattingly, Jenny, *Volunteers in Museums and Art Galleries*, Volunteer Centre UK, 1984, p.58.

[13] Smith, Stuart B., 'Managing Volunteers, Spot the Difference', text of speech, Seminar on *Managing Volunteers in Museums*, Ironbridge Institute, (unpublished), 1987.

[14] Dovey, Bryan, National Museums Security Adviser, *Letter* 17/07/89.

[15] Hudson, Kenneth, 'The Flipside of Professionalism,' *Museums Journal*, March, 1989, pp.188–190.

[16] Kelly, Barbara, 'The Volunteer as Professional,' *News*, AAMV, Winter, 1986.

[17] Handy, Charles, *The Future of Work*, Basil Blackwell, 1985 and *The Age of Unreason*, Business Books, 1989.

[18] Corfield, Michael; Keene, Suzanne, and Hackney, Stephen (eds) *The Survey: Conservation Facilities in Museums and Galleries*, United Kingdom Institute for Conservation (UKIC), 1989, p.74.

[19] Storer, J.D., *The Conservation of Industrial Collections. A Survey*, The Science Museum and Museums and Galleries Commission, 1989, p.25.

[20] Ramer, Brian, *A Conservation Survey of Museum Collections in Scotland*, Scottish Museums Council, 1989, p.74.

[21] Carlile, June, 'Friends as Volunteer Guides in Museums and Galleries. How do they function?' *Yearbook*, British Association of Friends of Museums, 1989–90, pp.58–59.

[22] Pearson, Anne, *Arts for Everyone. Guidance on Provision for Disabled*

People, Carnegie UK Trust and Centre on Environment for the Handicapped, 1985.

[23] Museums and Galleries Commission, *Museum Professional Training and Career Structure,* HMSO, 1987, p.26.

[24] Worts, Douglas, 'Professional Volunteers: A Contradiction in Terms,' *Museum Quarterly,* Winter, 1986, pp.8–15.

[25] Central Statistical Office, *Social Trends 20,* 1990 edition, HMSO, p.151.

3 | Policy Planning

*Thinking about management means thinking for ourselves. This is
often such hard work that we avoid it if we can in favour of less hard
work, like crisis management.*
NCVO News, February, 1989

Volunteer Policy—Why is it needed?

Recognition of the validity of volunteer activity and all-volunteer museums as
a major aspect of museum provision throughout the United Kingdom means
that trustees, governing bodies and management committees, on the one hand,
and senior managers, keepers and curators on the other, must address the specific issues relating to the management of volunteers within any corporate plan.
The formulation of a policy on volunteer involvement is essential for all
museums where volunteers are present.

A volunteer policy clarifies the position of volunteers in relation to the main
goals of a museum or gallery in the broad context of staffing policies. In small,
self-managed, all-volunteer museums—or those with one paid curator/man-
ager—for the most part, the volunteer policy will be synonymous with overall
management policy. In museums where volunteer activity is extensive, consideration needs to be given to constructing a policy on volunteers that dovetails
with existing management policies and existing management structures. In
many cases, this will involve undertaking a policy review to examine the present
volunteer policy. It will mean looking at supervisory arrangements, especially
the relative merits of appointing a volunteer co-ordinator either on a paid or
unpaid basis, and exploring the benefits of producing a manual or handbook
on policy and procedures for the use of volunteers and volunteer managers.

As the partnership between the museum and volunteer becomes established
practice in the 1990s, conditions of service become increasingly important.
Volunteers are more aware of their rights: they are developing high expectations. The regulation and standardisation of procedures and practices is formal recognition by an organisation of its responsibilities for the quality of
volunteer performance and the personal development volunteers themselves.
Voluntary organisations within the field of social services present a marked
contrast to museums. The Citizens Advice Bureau (CAB), Relate and The Samaritans are highly structured, have cohesive policies, strict selection procedures
and printed codes of practice.

A series of ad hoc arrangements, it can be argued, allows for flexibility
and avoids bland compromise and standardisation. It allows for individual
motivation and a response to the uniqueness of the situation within a particular
museum. Such a position is supported by the knowledge that voluntary tasks
are often best accomplished by small, decentralised teams with their own base
and identity from which to function. But the absence of policies means that the
potential of volunteers and the complexity of managing them go unrecognised.

Questions concerning the recruitment, induction and training of volunteers;

employment law and liability and working relations are common to large and small museums alike whether they are national, local authority or independent. So too, is the need for a dialogue and consultation process amongst interested parties in the formulation of volunteer policy.

Identify the Type of Organisation—Who decides volunteer policy?

The answer to the question: 'Who decides volunteer policy?' will be different for each museum. It is important to identify what type of organisation the museum is; what kind of management structure it has and what kind of 'culture' it fosters in order to decide exactly who should be involved in formulating policy on volunteers. (Figure 1)

There are three broad categories of voluntary organisations corresponding approximately to the three different organisational structures outlined under the heading 'Independent' in Figure 1. First, 'mutual support'—many small, all-volunteer, local history museums are set up by their members to meet their own immediate needs. These organisations are inward looking and operate on an informal, networking basis. They are run by a committee and secretary. Second, 'campaigning'—many industrial and transport museums started in this way, led by committees of Friends or Supporters groups. Some of these small museums set up by conservation enthusiasts, Civic and Amenity Societies or Friends Associations remain small voluntary bodies and some take on the status of unincorporated charitable trusts. Others, including the large independent museums that are neither privately owned nor run by a company, fall into the third category of voluntary organisation—'service delivery'. The majority of these are charitable trusts set up as companies limited by guarantee. They offer a publicly orientated service to meet variously the demands of tourists, school parties and the local community. Paid staff work alongside volunteers or, alternatively, volunteers work alongside paid staff.

In voluntary museums in the independent sector management committees and trustees play an important role in policy planning. There is a sliding scale. In small, all-volunteer museums members of the management committee or trustees are more involved in the running of the museum on a day to day basis than when there is a large core of paid staff. (Contrast Case Studies 3 & 5) In these museums, and national and large local authority museums in the public sector, volunteer policy planning is undertaken by paid staff.

Whether management committees or paid curators/managers take the initiative in policy planning, what is important is that all interested groups and individuals are identified and consulted over the formulation of volunteer policy. Some, or all, of the following participants should be included—volunteers, paid staff, the volunteer organiser, trade union representatives and members of the Friends Association. This consultation process is essential. It gives coherence to volunteer policy planning whilst maintaining the ethos of volunteering.

A Policy Review—How can it help?

A policy review creates a firm foundation for policy planning. Difficulties arise in policy planning because few museums remain in a static position. The organ-

Figure 1

What Kind of Organisation is Your Museum?

Independent

Voluntary
(a) 'Mutual Support':
Committee: Secretary;
Membership subscription; all-volunteer.

(b) 'campaigning': Committee:
sub-committees; leader/manager;
Membership subscription &
donations: volunteer/paid help.

(a) & (b) are sometimes
unincorporated Charitable
Trusts: trustees take personal
liability for the
society/association

(c) 'service delivery': Charitable
Trust; Incorporated Company:
trustees limited liability; Board,
'core' paid staff, volunteers:
plural funding—local
authority/sponsorship admission
charges: Friends Associations.

Private
— Individual Ownership;
— Company Ownership

National

Trustees: Grant-in-aid from the
government: Director-paid staff:
limited support from volunteers;
Friends or Members
Associations.

University

(large) Board reporting to the
government body of the
university: direct funding Univ.
Funding Council;
Curator/Director-paid staff;
limited volunteer support;
Friends Associations.

Local Authority

Committee of Elected
Councillors; direct funding—
community charge;
Director/curator—paid staff;
limited volunteer support (except
in small museums); Friends
Associations.

Note:

1. Managing bodies of *all* museums are volunteers.

2. Some trustees wear two hats. They act in a decision making
   capacity on the board and in an 'active' hands-on capacity in the
   museum.

3. In planning policy for volunteers working in the museum on a day
   to day basis gaining support from and using the expertise of
   trustees in a consultative capacity is important.

isational flexibility of museums in the independent sector that allows a quick
response to changing circumstances also means that regular policy reviews are
necessary. In the public sector, a re-assessment of the role of volunteers in
supporting paid staff necessitates an evaluation and co-ordination of their current contribution.

The steps that need to be taken in a policy review are listed in Figure 2. They take account of the needs of museums in the independent and public sectors. Calculations concerning the number of volunteers required, space needed, a breakdown of the costs and details of supervision and training arrangements are common to all museums.

A review helps an organisation to understand who does volunteer, who might volunteer and whether their skills and talents are being used fully and effectively. (Chapter 2, p 21) The potential source of supply of volunteers will vary according to geographical area and demographic trends. It is not possible for small museums in rural areas in the north of England, Scotland and Wales to be as selective about recruitment as those in the South East or South West of England. (Case Study 5) They have to make the best use they can of the skills and talents available within the community. Training, therefore, becomes increasingly important. Moreover, different types of collections will attract different types of volunteer. (Compare Case Studies 1, 4, 8 & 9)

Figure 2

Policy Review

How do volunteers help the museum/gallery achieve its goals? Is their contribution effective?
(To be undertaken either before the start of a volunteer programme or when revising volunteer policy.)

- ' explore the ways in which the volunteer contribution interlocks with the management plan and organisational structures.

- examine and define areas where volunteers work and tasks undertaken. Are these 'core' or supplementary activities?

- calculate/estimate the numbers of volunteers working/required.

- investigate the supervision arrangements in relation to the line management structure of the organisation and staff time—curator/manager, volunteer co-ordinator.

- examine procedures and practices—recruitment, induction and training.

- look at potential supply—density and employment profile of surrounding population, accessibility of site, demographic trends.

- assess the resources—office/common room space, transport, equipment, workspace for special projects, expenses and training.

- explore funding requirements and funding sources—Friends, sponsorship.

- formulate a volunteer policy through consultation between curators/managers, volunteers, the volunteer organiser, members of the Friends Association and Trade Union representatives.

The three main areas where major differences will occur between all-volunteer museums and museums with up to two paid staff, on the one hand, and the large independent, local authority and national museums, on the other, are in:-

• the role of management committees and trustees

• the role of the Friends/Supporters

• the identification of 'core' and support tasks

A volunteer policy review in these areas is critically important as part of the management of change. For those museums in the process of expansion, transition to charitable trust status, or starting to supplement direct funding or grant-in-aid with earned income and sponsorship, a review can pinpoint where changes are needed in terms of the volunteer contribution to meet fresh goals and new challenges. It is more difficult for individual volunteers to see a decision that involves a change in, or the complete removal of their status, as a personal slight if the change in the direction of volunteer policy is the result of a review.

Management Committees and Boards of Trustees

Traditions and entrenched positions are rapidly established in any organisation. In the voluntary sector as a museum grows in size, and appoints paid staff in increasing numbers, the role of the management committee alters too. A reluctance to relinquish control by individuals who have dedicated hours of their own time to building up the museum is understandable. Tasks that need to be delegated to paid staff who are present on a daily basis need to be identified and re-evaluated in a series of regular reviews as the organisation continues to expand. This process inevitably involves a certain loss of control by the management committee. Sometimes the 'culture' and democratic character of a campaigning organisation is retained. (Case Study 4) At other times—and more generally—the balance of decision making is moved from the original volunteer component to paid staff. The Board of Trustees then acts principally in a supportive role and acts in an executive capacity only on major policy decisions. Trustees of national museums have an expanding role as changes in the management policies and management structures of these organisations are ratified and implemented.

Friends Associations

Friends are often responsible for setting up and running a museum in the independent sector. However, they operate mainly in a fund-raising and public relations role in the public sector and sometimes offer services such as guiding. The autonomy of Friends Associations means that they can easily become separated from the main body of the organisation. (Appendix III) A review can highlight the issues that arise as a result of expansion, changes in the management structure of the museum or a re-assessment of the role of the Friends Association and help to circumvent potential problems. In some museums contact is maintained by the automatic appointment of the Chairman of the Friends Association onto the Board of Trustees. In other museums the attitude of the Director is crucial in integrating the work of Friends Associations into the work of the museum as a whole. (Case Study 2) In one museum a Code of Conduct for members of the Society of Friends clearly states their position when they volunteer to give practical help: 'All members working on behalf of the Museum must act strictly under the instructions of the responsible member of the permanent staff'.

'Core' and Support Tasks

A review can examine the effectiveness of the inter-relationship between the museum's goals and the identification of 'core' and support functions in the context of volunteer policy. As museums in the voluntary sector start to employ paid staff decisions as to what museum functions are 'core' functions and who should do them need to be taken. Most museums moving in this direction begin by appointing either a paid curator or a project manager. Specialist conservation skills are bought on a consultancy basis and preventive conservation continues to be done by volunteers. Paid seasonal staff and volunteers operate visitor reception facilities. Guiding is generally undertaken by Friends in both the independent and public sectors and a large proportion of documentation and research is also done by volunteers. Friends sometimes run the Information Desks in national museums. Should better care of collections and increased access to collections mean an expansion of volunteer activity in these areas? Are volunteers the best means of service delivery? If so, questions concerning the way volunteers are viewed within the organisation as far as 'core' and support tasks are concerned, as well as training, become issues of paramount importance in volunteer policy planning.

A Volunteer Organiser—Is someone needed?

There are immense advantages in employing a volunteer organiser or volunteer co-ordinator on a paid or unpaid basis. (Case Studies 3, 8, 9) For all museums the fragmentation of the volunteer effort can present problems. Maintaining good communications and ensuring that volunteers receive up-to-date information is difficult when people come in on a rota system only once a week or once a fortnight, at weekends, or for a week once or twice a year. It is significant that in those museums cited as examples of good practice in Appendix I, the majority employ a volunteer organiser or co-ordinator. Even in those museums where procedures and practices are fully in place communication remains a critical issue. (Case Study 5) Up to seven volunteers are needed to offer services equivalent to one full-time member of staff.

The quantity of volunteers, the reciprocal nature of the agreement between the volunteer and the museum together with an array of disjointed timetables means that a high level of organisation is essential. (Figure 3) The supervision of a task can remain with individual members of the paid staff or project leaders once the parameters for the work have been negotiated between the volunteer organiser, curator/team leader and the volunteer. (Case Study 8a) A volunteer organiser or co-ordinator can encourage teamwork and foster positive working relations through providing training, setting aside time to talk to people, offering encouragement and praise and, if necessary, carrying out disciplinary procedures.

Procedures and Practices—What is required?

A loose-leaf manual or printed handbook is important in establishing the status of volunteers within the organisation and necessary when questions concerning

Figure 3

Volunteer Co-ordinator

Does the museum need a volunteer co-ordinator (paid or unpaid) to assist with the transfer of policy into action through the following tasks?

- liaison   * volunteer and curatorial staff
  -        * public relations, Friends, open days, edit a newsletter/journal

- programme planning

- job design and job descriptions—with curators/managers

- preparing a recruitment and skills register

- induction and training:
  'core'   * general information and tour of the museum/gallery
               * safety/security
  'task specific' * skills for the job
               * awareness training on volunteers for paid staff

- organise supervision and reporting arrangements for volunteers

- organise volunteer support and development, including clerical help, access to a telephone and career paths

- organise volunteer records and evaluation/appraisal procedures

- offer recognition to volunteers through—the personal touch, awards, and social gatherings

- negotiate disciplinary/dismissal proceedings

insurance, dismissal and the payment of expenses arise. Once decisions have been reached as to how, where and in what ways volunteers can help a museum to achieve its goals, a policy statement can be made openly available. This, together with information on the museum and volunteer projects, application forms, details of the volunteer agreement and codes of practice can be included in the manual. (Figure 4)

Although a volunteer agreement, guidelines for the volunteer and codes of practice can be put together in one general package, this detracts from the clarity of purpose of each aspect of the arrangement. Separate documents offer greater precision and, in turn, this leads to a greater degree of accountability in the relationship between the volunteer and the museum.

Figure 4

Policy and Procedures Manual Handbook

Does the museum need a manual/handbook in which to assemble and co-ordinate relevant information in loose-leaf form for easy up-dating? This would include some or all of the following:-

- Information on the organisation—background, aims and objectives.

- Policy Statement on Volunteers.

- Details on Volunteer Programme/Programmes, including job descriptions/application forms.

- Volunteer Agreement.

- Recruitment, Induction, Training procedures.

- Codes of Practice e.g. Health and Safety, Disciplinary Procedures.

- Insurance.

- Reimbursement of Expenses.

4 Policy Implementation

Staff in other museums complain that volunteers take so much time to instruct that it is easier to do the job oneself. That is not our experience: we love them
Private View, Dulwich Picture Gallery Newsletter, Autumn, 1989

I: Recruitment and Recognition

Volunteers' needs, expectations and skills should be in step with organisational requirements. Often there is the feeling that a volunteer should never be turned away, even though a suitable job is not available, and that all offers of help must be used. Jobs have even been created especially for a volunteer rather than recruiting a suitable person for a specific task.

Recruitment

A curator, manager or volunteer co-ordinator should be designated or appointed to follow recruitment and selection procedures through from advertisement to appointment.

Checklist: Recruitment

- Advertising arrangements—Friends groups, word of mouth, media, community groups and newspapers.

- Job description—including task specification.

- Application form—including skills, previous experience, availability, transport needs.

- Interview—conducted by curator/manager, volunteer co-ordinator or small team.

- Recruitment checks—including references.

- Equal opportunities monitoring.

Advertising

Informal networking—word of mouth advertising—can be extremely effective. The dangers are, however, that current volunteers will recruit in their own image. If volunteering in museums is to be made attractive to a wider audience, then new, innovative recruitment methods are needed. This includes advertising on local radio, in the local newspaper, at youth clubs, job centres and in the specialist newspapers of ethnic minorities and people with disabilities. (Equal

Opportunities p 40) It also includes recruiting through 'networking' i.e. using local voluntary organisations and community groups.

Job Design and Job Description

Job Design

Tasks are part of the 'package' which may attract volunteers. The person responsible for designing jobs must know why volunteers are needed, what aspects of the work will be delegated to them, and how they will be supervised. If this is a volunteer co-ordinator s/he will need to work in close consultation with the curator/manager who will act as supervisor.

Different kinds of jobs demand different levels of commitment and some volunteers want routine tasks because of time limitations, family responsibilities or a low level of self-confidence. Other volunteers are prepared to work with a higher level of responsibility and commitment. For retired professional people it is often erroneous to assume they will apply expertise gained in a paid capacity when they offer their services as a volunteer. An accountant or teacher, for example, might want to transfer her/his skills to a new area of work.

Consideration needs to be given as to how each job fits into the organisational structure and lines of management. A voluntary post should not replace a paid post. How does it fit in with the organisation's overall policy on volunteers? Is there room for the personal development of the volunteer within this job or will the experience gained allow the volunteer to move on to another task? If these questions are resolved satisfactorily, and time allocations are decided on to suit both paid staff and volunteer, then a firm foundation is established for volunteer work that is central and not tangential to a museum's goals.

Checklist: Job Design

- Is the job needed?
- How does the job contribute to the museum's goals and volunteer policy?
- Why should a volunteer do it? If the answer is "for financial reasons", have a serious re-think. A voluntary post should not replace a paid post. The aim is to supplement, not supplant paid staff.
- Do the specific duties allocated to each job allow the volunteer room for individual development and a career path?
- Does the job fit the time frame of the volunteer?
- Are the specific policies and procedures involved understood by staff and volunteers?
- Does it constitute humane, interesting work, providing satisfaction, a sense of belonging and a chance to learn?

Job Description

A job description gives specific information on the scope and remit of a particular task. Like Job Design it should be developed by the person responsible for volunteers in consultation with the curator/manager under whose supervision the volunteer will work. Job title, principal purpose, duties and responsibilities of the post should be stated along with what potential it offers for the volunteer. The skills, knowledge and/or experience desirable or required must also be laid down together with details of lines of accountability. The job description is separate from a volunteer agreement.

Example:
Avon Wildlife Trust—Job description:

Practical Workday Co-ordinators

The Task
This post requires people to draw up regular lists of workdays on our reserves with the help of the Conservation Officer. Some liaison with our reserve wardens will also be necessary.

The schedules produced then have to be distributed to all our practical volunteers. Volunteers are also needed to load up the van for the Sunday work-day preferably on the preceding Friday.

Requirements
A chance to put your organisational skills to good use! A knowledge of practical conservation would be useful. Some experience of word-processing would be helpful, although training could be provided.

Time Involved
The production and posting of the workday schedule takes about half a day, although complications can make the job a little longer. This would be done every two or three months. The loading of the van would be once a week and take about an hour each Friday prior to a workday. Again this job could be shared amongst several people.

Location
All work is currently based at Trust Headquarters. However, some of the more specialist tools may have to be collected from other stores in the future.

Applications

The main purpose of an application form is to obtain information from potential volunteers to make effective placements. A well-designed application form, however, can provide the basis for a skills register and record keeping: it can also help subsequently with evaluation procedures. Apart from basic personal data, room can be provided for information on time available, skills and expertise, interests, preferred areas of work and recruitment checks e.g. referees, special considerations e.g. access requirements and dietary needs. (Figure 5)

Interview and Selection

The interview is a two-way learning process. Even at those museums placed in locations where volunteers are at a premium the interview is important. It may be formal or informal. It provides an opportunity for the potential volunteer to find out about the place, staff and other volunteers as well as details of the nature of the work on offer. Careful selection and matching of the volunteer's

Figure 5

The following information is requested in order to process your application and will also be used for appropriate administrative purposes. PLEASE TYPE OR PRINT

PLEASE USE REVERSE SIDE TO: provide a brief statement of your objectives in seeking an assignment through this program
elaborate on your response to questions below

Mr( )   Mrs( )
Ms( )   Miss( )_____ Date _____

Home Address _____

 City _____ State _____ Zip _____

Home Phone (   ) _____ Business Phone (   )_____ Date of Birth _____

(1) Education (indicate school, university or college; degree(s); and major field(s) of study): _____
_____
_____

(2) Business/Volunteer Experience _____
_____
_____

Title of last position _____
Name of immediate supervisor _____ Telephone (   )_____
Kind of business/organization (manufacturing, accounting, social services, etc.) _____
Have you ever had a background check by the Federal Government? Yes _____ No _____
Have you ever held a security clearance?   Yes _____ No _____
(3) Special interests _____
_____

Skills: Typing _____ Word Processor _____ Computer _____ Other _____

Languages

(other than English)	Speaking Ability			Written Translations					
				into English			from English		
	exc.	good	fair	exc.	good	fair	exc.	good	fair
_____									
_____									
_____									

Availability: Indefinite: (1 year or more) _____ Short Term: (3–6 months) _____ (1–3 months) _____
If short term, indicate inclusive dates: from _____ to _____
Day(s) per week (please circle):   Mon.   Tues.   Wed.   Thurs.   Fri.
Hours per day _____
Total hours per week _____
In case of emergency, contact _____ Relationship _____ Phone (   ) _____
Please name the specific radio station, newspaper article, individual or other source through which you hears about this volunteer program: _____
_____

Applicant's Signature _____ Social Security No. _____
OFFICE USE ONLY   Date Acknowledged _____
BVP FL1/26

interests, skills and enthusiasms to an available job creates the foundation for an effective, co-operative team. (Appendix III, VAMI)

Whether there is a single interviewer, such as the Volunteer Co-ordinator, or a team an interview record form may be useful. This also provides data for record keeping afterwards. Open-ended questions encourage volunteers to talk about themselves as well as giving the interviewers an opportunity to find out about their motivation and commitment.

If the person is suitable references can be taken up and other recruitment checks can be done. If a candidate is rejected, a letter of thanks saying they will be informed of future opportunities is important in maintaining good community relations. Other opportunities for voluntary work in the locality can be suggested.

Recruitment Checks

Checks should be incorporated into a museum's recruitment and selection procedures. They can be made part of the application form. Checks that may be carried out in addition to taking up references include an investigation into a volunteer's driving licence and insurance status; health and past offences. One argument against such action is that excessive red tape can discourage volunteers. Frequently, however, the reverse is true. The volunteer is reassured by the care taken by the museum thus demonstrating that s/he is suitable to hold a position of responsibility.

Checklist: Recruitment Checks

Permission from a volunteer to carry out these checks is required.

Screening is controversial. It is a precaution against special risk—a necessary *final* check and should not be used in a routine investigation.

- *References*
  Take up references
  Prepare a simple pro-forma to send to referees
  If a person has been referred by another organisation e.g. the Volunteer Bureau they may already have references

- *Driving Licence*
  Valid driving licence
  Insurance
  — use of a vehicle may constitute 'change of use'
  — prepare a standard letter for the insurance company from the museum to confirm that cover is satisfactory
  — prepare a declaration that there is no medical reason to prevent a volunteer from driving

- *Health*
  At interview ascertain what tasks would be unsuitable e.g. heavy lifting/heart condition
  Consultation with the volunteer's doctor, if necessary, and only with permission

- *Screening for particular activities*
  Handling money. Disclosure of criminal offences is required for all volunteers handling money. This includes spent offences as defined by the *Rehabilation of Offenders Act*, 1974.
  All volunteers, especially those who will be involved in contact with vulnerable groups, i.e. mentally handicapped/elderly, should be carefully interviewed and references obtained for them.
  Work with children. Potential volunteers who will have substantial, unsupervised access to children must disclose all criminal convictions including any spent offences (as above).

— A pilot scheme, to be evaluated in 1991, is currently under way in Lancashire and Dudley, and nationally for voluntary agencies which have a national recruiting structure, whereby volunteers may be checked by the National Identification Bureau. Access is currently restricted to participating organisations; no decision on the extension of the pilot will be made before late 1991.
— Checks may be made with the Department of Social Services (DSS) Consultancy Service register of those with resignation/dismissals or major convictions relating to child care work.
— Department of Education and Science (DES) List 99 contains details of people not allowed to be employed as teachers or youth workers.

NB Some voluntary organisations see screening these volunteers by police checks as a serious threat to civil liberties. Others see it as essential for the protection of children under 16 years. The most serious offences are sexual, violence or drug offences.

The Home Office and the Volunteer Centre UK support the screening of volunteers where it would apply to paid staff, but stress that it should be done only when deemed necessary and with sensitivity and compassion. A rule may be to consider confidential precautions of this nature as reasonable if they help prevent the risk of a claim of negligence.

Equal Opportunities

In 1985 the Equal Opportunities Commission—set up to regulate employment discrimination based on race, religion and sex—recommended a code of practice which is not mandatory, but must be taken into account in any proceedings under the Sex Discrimination Act, 1975. Although this is not legally binding, it recommends that thought be given to reviewing current practices and procedures and to job opportunities, voluntary or otherwise.

If the museum has an equal opportunities policy this affects not only recruitment procedures like job design and application forms, but also health and safety, insurance and training matters. The aim is one of positive action in promoting equal opportunities in practices and service provision for volunteers as well as for paid staff. A commitment to anti-racism and anti-sexism can be asked of all volunteers. A complaints procedure should be available to deal with such matters as sexual harassment.

Minority Groups

Despite a growing awareness of the needs of members the black and ethnic communities and disabled people in the museum profession as a whole and the creation of specially-funded museum posts in Leicester and Bradford, few volunteer or join supporters' clubs. Even where these groups represent a high proportion of the population, the evidence suggests that active volunteer involvement is minimal and limited to help on an occasional basis.

Ethnic Groups
Manchester Jewish Museum is one amongst a small number of isolated examples of well co-ordinated programmes. In the United States Neighbourhood Museums are sometimes satellites of the main museum. Anacostia is an outpost of the Smithsonian Institution in a principally black neighbourhood.

Here there is a highly developed programme of black volunteers. But the Smithsonian Institution experiences similar problems to those of British museums in central Washington where there are few black volunteers in a city where the majority of the population is black. Through special exhibitions a conscious attempt is made to reach out to the black community. One at the Renwick Gallery on 'Slave Quilts of the Ante-Bellum South' in 1989 did attract black volunteer demonstrators.

Disability Groups
Little is known of the extent and nature of the work of disabled volunteers in museums in the United Kingdom. Yet, in terms of numbers and age range people with disabilities represent a huge untapped source of voluntary help. One in ten people in the United Kingdom has a disability. They are available since many cannot undertake full-time paid employment or otherwise their social security benefits would be adversely affected. Carers of people with disabilities are another possible source of volunteers.

Special recruitment methods to reach people with disabilities are required. These include local disability organisations, education authorities, youth workers, careers officers and job centres. In addition, links can be made across volunteering boundaries. Some volunteers, able-bodied or otherwise, volunteer in both the social services and cultural spheres, but rarely are their experiences cross-fertilised to the benefit of both organisations. For example, a local Volunteer Bureau with a volunteer hospital drivers scheme could use the scheme to take blind or visually impaired volunteers to a local museum instead.

Volunteers with disabilities offer another dimension to the museum's activities. They enrich the experience for all. Not only can these volunteers translate feedback on the needs of volunteers with disabilities into positive action, but they can also advise on provision for visitors with similar disabilities. They can arrange guides for blind or visually-impaired people and provide help with specific skills such as braille and lip-reading. They can operate public relations and outreach programmes by taking exhibits to people in residential homes, hospitals or day care centres. In short, they can provide time and resources to enable the museum to meet some of the special needs of the community.

Offer of Appointment and Volunteer Agreement

Once a volunteer is recruited a letter of appointment should then be sent out. Some museums also send out a welcome letter together with a written agreement outlining the conditions of service to be signed by the volunteer. This Agreement or Contract is legally binding but it should not be confused with a Contract of Employment. This cannot be used in relation to volunteers (Chapter 4II, p. 49).

Checklist: Volunteer Agreement

- Clarification of the volunteer's role, tasks and time commitment.

- Details of the position/person to whom the volunteer is accountable.

- Information on personnel practices—details of induction, training and support, procedures for illness and holidays, grievance or disciplinary procedures.

- Insurance provision.
- Expenses allowable and arrangements for payment.
- Health and Safety procedures.
- Working arrangements and conditions.
- Expectations of the volunteer—punctuality, courtesy, commitment, regular attendance, a satisfactory performance of the agreed task and willingness to undertake training.
- Specify a trial period e.g. 6 months, and request a period of notice in the case of resignation.

When a volunteer signs an agreement before starting work, there are two way advantages. If the volunteer proves unsuitable for reasons of absenteeism, or an inability to execute a particular task, the appointment can be reviewed. Equally, if the museum does not fulfil its obligations, a volunteer is in a position to file a complaint. Termination of the agreement is a last resort. In this case, however, a period of notice built into the agreement and a fixed term letter of appointment are helpful.

Records of Volunteer Experience

Records of a volunteer's personal details, skills and experience whilst working at the museum should be kept from the moment volunteers are appointed until the day they leave. Recognition should be given to volunteers who have acquired skills as a result of training. If records are kept well they provide data for evaluating the volunteer programme as a whole and material for a personal reference when a volunteer leaves the museum.

Checklist: Records of Volunteer Experience
- A copy of the application form.
- Interview notes and impressions.
- A copy of the job description and volunteer specification if such exist.
- Dates and times of specific activities, such as tasks undertaken, who the volunteer worked with, what was learned and if help was needed.
- Training should be outlined and copies of certificates of completion e.g. for technical skills, should be included.
- Description of skills learned and the strength of them e.g. named machines or equipment, speed and accuracy.
- Record of any evaluation carried out.
- Copies of any awards.
- Examples of work e.g. visual material such as exhibition photographs.
- References from the supervisor or volunteer co-ordinator which will include some of the above and an assessment of development based on discussion, interview, record cards, diaries or log books.

Induction

Introducing new volunteers to their surroundings can be done through a formal tour and talk about the organisational structure of the museum and how their own contribution fits in. An Induction Pack is provided by some organisations. (Appendix III,A,3) A warm welcome is critical to a successful volunteer input. This introduction should be followed up by a briefing on fire, safety and security procedures, on the one hand, and information on social activities on the other.

Recognition

In-service Development and Support

The scant attention paid to stimulating and sustaining volunteer involvement in museums is out of keeping with the rising demand for the services of volunteers. A good staff development policy offers opportunities for volunteers to develop interests and skills alongside paid staff. Training programmes, regular appraisal of work in progress and a deliberate policy of recognition through rewards and social gatherings provide the necessary ongoing system of support and encouragement. Moreover, they are fundamental to maintaining high, professional standards of service within museums. Grievance procedures and disciplinary measures ensure that when a problem does occur it can be dealt with quickly and effectively.

Motivation

For volunteers motivation is a form of private agenda. It includes a volunteer's own goals and expectations, for altruistic or other reasons such as self-esteem, an expression of personal values, social affiliation, academic credit, work experience, or exploring career opportunities. Reciprocity is recognised more and more as the basis for most volunteering. The Volunteer Centre UK's research 'On Volunteering: Motivation, Images and Experiences' (1990) demonstrates the range of volunteer motivation and the difference in motivation between those volunteering for the first time and those who have already been involved in voluntary work.

Training

On the whole, structured training provision has been limited to activities such as guiding or preventative conservation through organisations such as NADFAS. Most volunteers have no knowledge or previous experience of the tasks they agree to do and paid staff find supervision time prohibitive. Ad hoc on the job training has, in the past, led to resentment and frustration on both sides. This situation is changing. The newly established Museum Training Institute has the training of volunteers as one of the three main platforms of its programme.

Basic 'core' training is also part of risk management and safety procedures.

A court would not be critical of a volunteer displaying a lower standard than a paid person in a particular field, but guidance to the degree of reasonable skill would be expected. This includes:- the safe handling of special tools and equipment; hazard awareness training and ensuring a volunteer understands her/his own limitations and when to seek assistance.

A Training Programme

The cost of training is frequently ignored in any review of resources for the implementation of a volunteer policy. Induction, on the job training, in-service training and refresher courses are essential if the volunteer contribution is to be effective within the museum and also a satisfying experience for the volunteers. Standardisation is difficult. The variety of museum collections and management structures as well as the different ways in which volunteers interlock into the activities of paid staff, or operate on a self-management basis, means that training programmmes are ideally custom-made to suit the particular needs of an individual museum.

Attaching a volunteer to an overloaded curator/manager can hinder work in progress rather than offering training opportunities. However, if this aspect of the curator's work is built into his/her job description and time is allocated for this task—for example, one morning a week—then such specific, tailor-made training can be extremely effective. In addition, a cascade system can be put into operation. The person trained carefully by the curator/manager can then train an additional volunteer that s/he has acquired. In turn, this means that the curator/manager need only monitor standards and offer occasional additional help rather than take half a day out of every working week.

A variety of in-service provision is available. Training courses are provided by the Museums Association, The Association of Independent Museums (AIM) and the Area Museum Councils as well as organisations like the Ironbridge Institute and the Volunteer Centre UK. The Area Museum Councils have recently appointed Training Officers and offer advice and courses of direct local relevance. One area where training is highly structured and organised is that of internships. Traditionally the method of entry into the museum profession is to undertake volunteer work and then an internship during a course of graduate or postgraduate study. (Case Study 1, Chapter 2, p. 22)

Training is not only required for volunteers working on the ground, but also for the supervising-curator/manager—or volunteer co-ordinator. The realisation that those managing volunteers need to be trained in specific skills, particularly in the area of managing inter-personal relationships, has led to the establishment of a Management Development Unit at the National Council for Voluntary Organisations. Other support is available from the Volunteer Centre UK. With the growth of the voluntary sector generally, managers need to address the implications of management without domination and without financial reward.

Monitoring, Appraisal and Evaluation

Trust is essential to co-operation. Volunteers may see evaluation processes as threatening rather than as useful planning tools which give them a stake in the organisation. It should be made clear that events and accomplishments are being evaluated, not people. Acknowledgement of progress can make people feel proud and successful. It also visibly demonstrates the importance of volunteer work. Evaluation shows that volunteers are accountable both externally and internally—to funding bodies and other staff. This helps to reduce the risk of volunteers being viewed as marginal to the organisation.

Omission of evaluation for volunteers is tantamount to separating volunteers from the rest of the workforce and implies that their work is incidental and of a lower status. To lower standards for volunteers is to do them a disservice since the only difference between them and paid staff is that they are rewarded through personal satisfaction and not through money.

Volunteer self-evaluation can take the form of written reports. However, this should not become an end in itself and people should not suffer from 'paralysis' when it has been completed. There is another danger with the evaluation process. Workers can be prevented from getting on with their jobs because they are being questioned all the time.

Checklist: Monitoring, Appraisal and Evaluation

- Applicants should be informed when they join a museum that evaluation will take place during training and that this will be followed by an occasional performance review.

- Evaluations should be developmental, not judgmental.

- A performance review should assess the volunteer's understanding of the goals, work, content and procedures involved in the task s/he is undertaking in the context of the museum as a whole. In turn, the volunteer should be encouraged to put forward suggestions or concerns.

- If a volunteer's performance is unsatisfactory, the reasons should be discussed and agreement reached on whether an alternative task would be more suitable.

Evaluation of Museum Volunteer Programmes

One way of bringing volunteers into the decision-making process, improving their self-confidence and finding out how to make better arrangements for them is to evaluate their programme.

Checklist: Evaluation of Museum Volunteer Programmes

- Clear goals: Are you aware of a statement of objectives for your museum? Are new volunteers given induction into the museum's philosophy and objectives?

- Adequate communications: Does information move upwards, downwards and across boundaries within the work environment?

- Adequate resources: How often do people meet as a team? Is there adequate provision in terms of your environment, management structure and training for you to do your job effectively and safely?

- Distribution of power: Can you influence the hierarchy? Do you make suggestions and, if so, are they heard and acted upon? Are there conflicts among staff?

- Efficient use of the resources/potential of the workforce: Do you feel that your organisation and its resources are used to the best advantage? Are you unclear about your role and what your responsibilities are? Are individual strengths and expertise fully utilised. Do you feel you learn, grow and contribute?

- Teamwork: Do you think staff work as a team? Do you get the opportunity to meet committee members and members of senior management?

- Morale: How well do staff respond to criticism? Is there commitment to the museum's work? Do you feel that you belong and are valued?

- Innovation: How often is planning discussed and by whom? Are new ideas encouraged or rejected and why? Have you set up any new activities or developments?

- Responsiveness: Is the museum involved enough in community activity? If not, why not? Does discussion take place with other organisations?

- Flexibility: Is there change to meet current trends? Are there enough opportunities for sufficient training?

- Problem-solving: What are the museum's problems? What is the system for changing them? Who should be consulted when problems arise and what should be done if something goes wrong?

Volunteer Rewards

Volunteers by the very nature of their motivation need positive and regular demonstration that their efforts are appreciated. A warm welcome, social gatherings, announcements of special achievements in the newsletter or local press and above all 'thank yous' are the kind of reward volunteers are seeking. Special facilities including car parking, creche, discounts on meals and goods bought in the shop are an added bonus. The National Trust gives volunteers a card for forty hours work which offers them free admission to Trust properties and a 10% discount in the shop. Outings to other museums have the dual benefits of a social gathering and cultural education.

Creating a Positive Climate for Volunteers:

Perhaps the most compelling reason volunteers have for staying at a museum is the feeling of belonging and contributing to it from within a working 'community'. Loyalty, interest and effort come from a sense of ownership and common purpose, shared planning, clarity of expectations, responsibility, progress and confidence in managers to give fair treatment and recognition. 'Leadership' style and the climate which a manager helps to create go hand-in-hand.

Checklist: Creating a Positive Climate for Volunteers

- Structure: whether loose and informal or highly regulated with rules and procedures.

- Responsibility: involving challenge and some autonomy, where possible, within tasks.

- Rewards: with an emphasis on the positive, rather than on punishment. There should be perceived fairness of policies and, for example, payment of expenses.

- Warmth: a feeling of good fellowship should be nurtured. The absence of cliques, good co-operation between paid staff and volunteers and friendly, informal social groups all contribute to this.

- Support: the perceived helpfulness of managers and others in the group is important. Emphasis should be on mutual support from above and below.

- Standards: the perceived importance of implicit and explicit goals and performance standards. These should be as high for volunteers as for paid staff.

- Responsiveness: the feeling that managers and other workers will listen to volunteer opinions. Problems should be brought out into the open and not ignored.

- Identity: a feeling of belonging to a group or team, and that a volunteer's contribution is valuable and valued.

Disciplinary Procedures and Dismissal

This is an area in which museums appear reluctant to exert authority. There is an embarrassment about what are considered to be difficult and sensitive areas. Nevertheless, they need to be addressed. Volunteers frequently expect more flexibility than paid staff in terms of defining their hours and work load. The need for flexibility has to be balanced with the need for accountability.

Checklist: Disciplinary Procedures

When a problem arises:-
- Check that the volunteer knew what was expected of her/him.

- Act promptly on day-to-day discipline, e.g. for unpunctuality.

- Be constructive rather than offering negative criticism. A change in a volunteer's schedule may prevent chronic lateness.

- When work is sub-standard suggest an alternative task.

- When necessary, institute procedures for misconduct.

Dismissal is never easy. If disciplinary measures have failed, however, or if performance is irredeemably inadequate, it may be in the volunteer's and organisation's best interests to terminate the appointment. Recalcitrant or disruptive attitudes can affect the morale of other personnel. Once the decision has been taken the matter must be dealt with speedily. There is no legal redress for the unjust dismissal of a volunteer.

Grievance Procedures, Resignation and Turnover

Resignation can occur because there are no official procedures for volunteer complaints. Volunteer workers have every right to make complaints or criticisms on any matter which causes them concern. This includes disagreement over duties, aspersions cast on character or allegations of dishonesty. In the first instance, they should raise the matter with their supervisor who should advise them of the complaints procedure. All complaints and grievances should be considered carefully and investigated fully, objectively and in a confidential manner.

Common causes of grievance and high turnover are a lack of support, direction and control in the work situation, poor treatment and poor working relations. The hostility of paid staff can aggravate problems and conflicts can arise between personal and organisational goals. Frequently, there is either too much work, or too little work, or too many difficult tasks. A lack of resources to accomplish goals leads volunteers to feel that they are not meeting expectations. When money is not a motivating factor recognition is all-important.

The appointment of a volunteer co-ordinator to look after all aspects of volunteer involvement can help to avoid 'turnover' for reasons such as the isolation or exploitation of the volunteer in low-level jobs which do not allow room for personal development. A volunteer co-ordinator or supervisor should learn to recognise the warning signs, including poor performance and indifference.

Good volunteers are accountable, but even good volunteers do not stay forever. Volunteers may choose to leave for any number of valid reasons such as family commitments, moving away from the area, or because they are no longer fit. When they leave it can cause disruption to tasks, but equally change can bring revitalization or end an excessive reliance on one person.

There should be a recognised procedure or mechanism to help volunteers feel that they are leaving legitimately without being put under pressure or treated as 'defectors.' Record-keeping, evaluation, monitoring and an established grievance procedure should ensure that most resignations do not come as a surprise for whatever reason . When some one decides to leave for good reason a reference should be offered by the supervisor or volunteer organiser. The volunteer should be thanked for her/his services.

II: Employment Law and Liability

This section looks at how employment law and liability affect volunteers working in museums. The legal obligations of an employer to paid staff derive from both common and statute law. The extent to which these laws offer protection to volunteers is examined. Where management initiative and management decisions are required to untangle and interpret aspects of the legislation that are 'grey areas' as far as volunteers are concerned, it is recommended that there is consultation within the organisation to reduce serious risk. On more specific legal matters, or if doubt remains, professional legal advice should be sought.

In larger museums, especially those in the public sector, questions concerning employment law and liability may be dealt with by personnel, administrative, legal or financial specialists on the staff. In smaller museums, the responsibility for understanding the issues relating to the legal liabilities of the organisation will be that of the curator/manager, or sometimes the volunteer organiser.

Volunteers and paid workers alike face problems of liability and insurance and require proper standards of recruitment and termination of contracts. It is clear, however, that legal doctrines are less well established for volunteers and that inadequate knowledge and confusion surround them. For example, the law is often unclear in stating whether it applies to both paid and unpaid personnel and there is much room for interpretation. Indeed, it could be said that it is as important for managers of volunteers to be aware of and to anticipate 'grey areas' as it is for them to follow the letter of the law when it is clearly stated.

Complications arise because an employer can be liable to an employee in contract law, but also under common law e.g. the law of tort of Negligence and Duty of Care. This will be discussed later. The parameters for voluntary activities laid down by a manager more, or less, strictly according to inclination, and a volunteer's deviation from them, may determine the degree of liability in the event of a negligence suit. The extent to which volunteer agreements and contracts are viewed as legally binding is a key issue.

Volunteer Agreements

The current interest and experimentation by a wide range of voluntary organisations, including some museums, with volunteer agreements and contracts reflects the belief that volunteers are most dependable when their contribution is well organised and well supported. An agreement not only governs the extent and nature of the commitment from the volunteer to the museum, but also the 'return' expected on the volunteer's gift of time from the museum in terms of administrative arrangements and support, training and rewards such as discount at the museum shop and the payment of out-of-pocket expenses.

Reciprocity forms the basis of all social relations and contracts. The essential difference in offering one's services by choice lies in motivation which goes beyond basic life obligations. When motivation is not primarily economic, the provision of other 'returns' becomes central to a successfully managed volunteer contribution and to establishing good working relations.

The Agreements or Contracts for volunteers that have been drawn up in museums so far have been devised to help establish good working relations and to provide procedures to deal with anticipated litigation. A preference for the term 'Volunteer Agreement' demonstrates the reservation and ambivalence surrounding the appropriateness of the term 'Contract' for volunteers working in museums. The Volunteer Centre UK has been advised that 'Agreement' rather than 'Contract' is the legally preferred term.

What needs to be understood by museum management and curators/managers is that there is a clear distinction between a contract and a contract of employment. A contract, or volunteer agreement, whereby each party has agreed to incur some minimum obligation will create, by definition, a legal relationship. It is a valid contract and legally binding. A contract of employment, however, does not depend on a written agreement for its validity. A contract of employment is legally binding when a 'worker' is being paid wages or other remuneration whether a written agreement has or has not been drawn up. In turn, this contract will attract employment protection legislation. (It should be noted that the term 'other remuneration' would not normally include the payment of expenses.) It follows, therefore, that a volunteer cannot enter into a contract of employment.

Whatever terminology is used—Agreement or Contract—the need for the clarification of mutual expectations and conditions of service remains. Agreements can be used to delimit legal responsibilities. Each party must be clear how loose the arrangement is since there are implications for legal liability. If benefits such as expenses, privileges, or promises to meet legal liabilities through particular insurance cover are included in a volunteer agreement then they should be seen as construing part of a contract for which an organisation is legally liable. If a museum has not made reciprocal promises there will not be a valid contract to enforce.

Circumstances will dictate the type of agreement required and some managers may not opt for one. Nevertheless, in all museums where volunteers are offering their services the subject should be given serious consideration before something goes wrong. When the museum wants to terminate the position of a volunteer or when the volunteer feels the victim of unfair treatment, the Volunteer Agreement becomes critically important.

Volunteers may enter into an agreement which is more, or less, strict. For example, the Samaritans are subject to strict obligations and discipline and they are held accountable for their actions. This is an illustration of the way in which volunteer accountability and organisational support are managed in a highly structured and successful manner in order to carry out work in an area of great sensitivity.

The Volunteer Centre UK has made recommendations that, at minimum, organisations should recognise an ethical contract which provides volunteers with proper management, clear expectations, training where appropriate, indemnity against reasonable risks and reimbursement of necessary expenses. Volunteers should receive treatment at least as fair as that given to paid workers and should be consulted on all major decisions. Effort should be made to remove unnecessary obstacles in law, taxation and income support.

Liability and Insurance

Recent evidence suggests that there is much uncertainty in museums over questions of liability, in its various forms, and the insurance cover required. In some instances, cover does not exist at all or is inadequate. There is considerable scope for a tightening up in provision and improved awareness of these issues.

Volunteers are as vulnerable as the rest of the workforce to risk. Yet, practice all too frequently fails to recognise this. Conditions in which volunteers work may be unacceptable or illegal, but there is often insufficient support to deal with these problems. A strong case can be made for integrating volunteers into the policies and provision made for paid staff.

The Employer's Liability (Compulsory Insurance) Act, 1969, states that an employer must insure her/his legal liability and a certificate should be publicly displayed. Legal liability exists quite independently of any insurance cover which may be arranged. If a museum is negligent, then it will be liable for the results of the negligence, irrespective of whether a volunteer or an employee is injured, or whether or not it is insured.

Insurance does not automatically cover volunteers. Some insurers, however,—for policy insurance purposes—are prepared to regard volunteers as employees. This means that they will cover the legal liability of the museum for volunteers as well as employees under the museum's Employer's Liability Policy. A suitable premium basis would have to be agreed. Agreeing to regard volunteers as employees for policy purposes does not alter their legal status. In the event of an accident insurers would deal with the claim on a strict liability basis. Several court cases held in the United States have applied the same conditions to unsalaried as to salaried workers where serious physical injury has been sustained.

Employers should also hold Public Liability insurance for employees and for the public using the premises or acting on their behalf. Volunteers should be informed whether they are to be treated as employees as far as Employer Liability and Public Liability cover are concerned. From the museum's point of view, it is preferable to treat the volunteers as employees and to arrange for the legal liability of the museum to be handled under the Employer's Liability and Public Liability Policies.

A museum does not necessarily have to accept liability for the results of the activities of volunteer staff carried out in good faith although it is advisable that it does so. In law, only if a volunteer is deemed to be acting as an agent of the museum is the museum liable for the negligence acts of a volunteer worker. There are, however, certain situations that could be regarded as 'grey areas':-

- a volunteer damaging museum property

- a volunteer injuring another volunteer or third party

- possible liability of a Friends group.

If the volunteers are regarded as employees for the purpose of the Employer's Liability and Public Liability Policies the first and second points are taken care of. (If a volunteer negligently injures another volunteer, this would be handled under the Employer's Liability Policy. If a volunteer injures a third party, this would be a Public Liability claim).

All insurance arrangements, including any personal accident cover, should be made clear to volunteers when they join the museum. Other insurance considerations relate to the museum's buildings, furniture and fittings, vehicles and collections.

Types of Liability

The Organisation's Negligence/'Duty of Care'

Liability derives from the common law of tort of Negligence and Duty of Care and applies in situations where individuals or organisations deal in a 'business' capacity with the public. It is in a museum's best interests as well as its duty to protect its volunteers. If a volunteer, employee or member of the public sustains injury or damage as a result of the museum's negligence, then a potential legal liability must follow. A museum may find itself liable if it can be shown that it failed to take 'reasonable care' to prevent injuries or damage. There is no automatic right to compensation. In the vast majority of accidents no compensation is ever paid.

Much depends on the circumstances of the accident and whether anyone acted negligently to cause it. A court's perception of the volunteer/client relationship and standards of competence is important. This includes, for example, failure by the museum to provide volunteers with timely information on potential hazards, uninspected equipment, a defective building or lighting. It also has implications for care in the selection of volunteers and the provision of adequate training, support and supervision, especially when someone is new to a task.

A break in the Health and Safety at Work Act (1974) may provide evidence of negligence in a civil action. There are obligations to be met as an occupier of buildings under this legislation. The injured party must show that, in the circumstances, there was a legal duty to take care of the safety of others, that negligent behaviour breached that duty and that damage resulted. There must be a close, 'direct' relationship between the two parties and risk has to be of the type that could be foreseen as a real risk and based on what could reasonably be known.

An employee injured at work is entitled to Social Security payments and s/he can also make a common law claim against her/his employer in the event of negligence. The volunteer, however, can only proceed against the negligent party. S/he will not be entitled to State benefits, including disablement benefit. If the museum is negligent, the volunteer—just as the employee—can make a claim. Compensation awarded by the Court will be the same whether an employee or volunteer is involved. This will vary according to the extent of the injuries, the amount of contributory negligence and the extent to which the museum is negligent.

The Volunteer's Negligence and 'Vicarious Liability'

Volunteers owe a duty of care to the people they deal with. If a volunteer is negligent and this results in injury, s/he is unlikely to be sued unless s/he is insured, even if s/he is proven to be directly at fault. This is because the rule of 'vicarious liability' makes an organisation liable by proxy.

The application of rule of 'vicarious' liability to volunteers depends on findings regarding the relationship of the museum and the volunteer. A museum will be liable for the negligence acts of a volunteer if

- there is a Contract of Service between the volunteer and the museum;

- the volunteer can be deemed in law to be acting as the agent of the museum;

- the museum ratifies the volunteer's negligent act.

With the exception of some 'semi-volunteers' who are paid a remuneration, museums will not be liable for the volunteer's negligent acts under the condition of Contract of Service. It is the payment of wages or other remuneration to the worker which determines whether there is a Contract of Service. Volunteers, by definition, are not paid wages.

Museums will be liable for the negligent acts of volunteers if they are deemed in law as acting as its agents. No contract between a museum and its worker is required in order for a volunteer to be regarded as acting as the museum's agent. In determining whether a volunteer is acting as the agent of a museum, the test is whether—at the time of the negligent act—s/he is acting within the scope of authority conferred on her/him. There is, however, a considerable degree of uncertainty in the law as to when a person will be deemed to be acting as agent of the other. The more a museum is in actual control over what the volunteer does and how s/he does it, the higher the chance that the volunteer will be deemed to be acting as the agent of the museum.

A museum can ratify the volunteer's negligent act. In this case the museum chooses to accept liability. It is important to distinguish between ratification where, in this context, a museum might accept liability, and the previous two categories where liability will be imposed on a museum if the circumstances outlined above exist.

The restriction of consideration concerning vicarious liability within a museum to employees shows inconsistent reasoning. It is quite possible that a court would find a volunteer, in practical terms, in the same position as a paid employee. A museum's potential liability for the civil wrongs of its volunteers should provide it with the impetus to exercise control over the jobs and tasks carried out by volunteers.

The Volunteer's Personal Liability

The lack of certainty surrounding the volunteer's position in regard to Negligence and 'Vicarious Liability' means that there are occasions when the museum may not be held liable for the actions of a volunteer worker. Damage to the property of, or injury to third parties, such as members of the public, or other workers—voluntary or paid—caused by a volunteer could conceivably remain the personal liability of the volunteer. So too, could the 'damage' caused by the faulty advice of a volunteer. It depends on whether the volunteer acted negligently and in what circumstances. Volunteers should be insured to the same extent as paid workers who carry out similar museum functions.

Insurance

Insurance is the only real method of protecting the museum and individuals in it against the risks outlined above. Curators/managers often complain that insurance for volunteers is too complicated. Frequently it is only taken seriously when something goes wrong. Museums should not be tempted to forego insurance on the grounds that accidents rarely occur, or that they can be dealt with by ex-gratia payments. A single major claim could bankrupt a museum. Neither is it sensible to cut corners on the cost of cover, because if it is not effective, museum managers could be liable.

Insurance is an important aspect of volunteer management and volunteer recognition. The case for taking out suitable and adequate insurance goes hand in hand with the practice of good risk management. This aims to reduce claims and keep premiums low. Training and supervision can often be improved, safety guidelines established and good personnel policies maintained.

Assumptions that insurance protection for volunteers is adequate or that cover has been arranged, should not be made without detailed investigations.

Check whether cover is for all foreseeable risks. In a new organisation consideration needs to be given to the nature and extent of the insurance cover required. The Volunteer Centre UK recommends that at minimum all volunteers should be covered for injury (Personal Accident) sustained during work and at least Public Liability insurance for third parties.

Insurance appropriate to individual tasks should be taken out. There can be no absolute rules, but a 'package' of policies can be discussed, depending on the circumstances, with a broker, company, private insurer, personnel office or solicitor. Negotiation may be necessary to meet the special requirements of transport, technological or 'open air' museums.

Methods of Cover

Provide a special policy for volunteers.
The National Trust, for example, covers volunteers for Public Liability insurance against a claim where negligence is proven. It also offers cover for Personal Accident using a sliding scale of benefits. This is designed to safeguard volunteers who are involved in a serious accident for which they are not liable. They do not insure a volunteer's personal equipment or personal possessions used on Trust premises.

Include or add volunteers to a basic policy covering paid staff at least for Public Liability.
This is frequently done in local authority museums by endorsing policies held in the council Treasurer's Department. These fulfil legal liabilities in relation to paid staff, but they can also include volunteers acting under the instructions of an officer of the council. Premiums are usually calculated on the basis of the number of employees and on salary levels. Many local authorities insure through their own Mutual Company and, in addition, look for other competitive bids. Provided volunteers are supervised they are usually covered for Employer's and Public Liabilities.

Join the 'umbrella' policy of a national organisation for its affiliated organisations or members.
- NADFAS has a blanket insurance policy covering Public Liability, 'All Risks'—which covers damage or loss to possessions of members or visitors—and Personal Accident. The owners of a property at which NADFAS Volunteer members are working must indemnify them against any third party claims, or for damage to articles on which they have agreed to work.

- BAFM has arranged an insurance scheme for Friends. This offers cover for Public Liability relating to all the activities of the group including social ones. It also covers the individual liability of members (whether volunteers or not) and 'member to member' liability. The Personal Accident cover applies to all the members of the group whether they are volunteers or not. It operates whilst members are engaged on Friends activities and offers benefits for death, loss of limb or eyes. A small hospital benefit is included but there is no weekly benefit.

- The Volunteer Centre UK promotes a scheme that covers Public Liability claims, bodily injury, damage to property, Personal Accident and Contingent

Liability. The latter is for groups working with motor vehicles. It is applicable provided that an effective motor insurance policy is in force. Mechanically-propelled vehicles or hazardous activity are excluded. This policy includes a no claims bonus and, for an additional premium, the loss of it.

Other arrangements exist such as government indemnity.

The government adheres to a non-insurance rule for grant-in-aid bodies and, therefore, national museums and galleries. This is sufficient cover unless there is a legal requirement to provide insurance, as for example with third party car insurance.

The rationale is that risks for which the government is liable are innumerable and widely distributed. It therefore benefits the Consolidated Fund to carry its own insurance, since premiums paid to an insurance company represent payment not only of the value of losses arising from the insured risk but also of a contribution to the expenses and profits of the company. It is deemed to be more cost-effective for the Fund not to insure and the Treasury will therefore allow no relaxation of the non-insurance rule.

This has caused concern in some national museums where it is felt that there is not sufficient clarification on matters such as liability for damage to museum goods, property and personal accident occasioned by volunteer involvement. This is judged to be particularly important since national museums are not permitted to take out commercial cover for damage to museum goods and property, or for Personal Accident.

Types of Cover

The categories of insurance that cover most eventualities are outlined below. Employer's Liability and Public Liability insurance have already been discussed. Special insurance for unusual or specialised activities, legal expenses insurance—covering possible prosecutions under acts such as the Health and Safety at Work Act—and legally compulsory insurance are not included.

Personal Accident Insurance

This provides payments, usually a lump sum and weekly payments over a stated period for bodily injuries or death, regardless of who is responsible. Cover may be excluded in certain cases, for example below and above certain age limits, or women within two months of the expected date of confinement.

Vehicle Insurance

All vehicle users are required by law to carry insurance that covers claims involving injuries and damage to people including passengers (Road Traffic Act, 1972). Nevertheless, if a volunteer wishes to use a private car, a policy holder must still inform the insurance company that s/he is using the vehicle as a volunteer to carry passengers.

It should be explained to the volunteer that written clearance should be obtained from the insurance company before s/he takes on a driving job. It is useful if the museum has a standard form or letter for volunteers to send to insurance companies. The policy should be up-to-date. Use must fall within the terms of policy and category of vehicle registration (whether or not a mileage allowance is being paid).

Comprehensive car insurance usually covers voluntary activities although this is not automatic. In some policies volunteer work can constitute a change of use. If the policy is not comprehensive it should be extended to cover 'business use' which is normally available, on request, at no extra charge. This extended use would only include driving as a specific part of a voluntary project. Travel from home to the workplace, as a general rule, would be covered by the existing policy. The volunteer should not commence work until confirmation of the extended cover has been received.

If the museum's own vehicles are used by volunteers, the museum is responsible for arranging appropriate insurance cover—at least third party. In the case of transport, technological or 'working' museums this may be a complex issue. It is wise for an organisation to effect a Contingent Liability policy. This guards against risk in the case of an accident for which the museum could be held responsible, regardless of vehicle ownership.

The museum must decide on the extent of cover it is willing to provide. For instance, policies are available to protect a volunteer's no claims bonus in case of mishap while volunteering.

Professional Indemnity

This protects a museum, if liable, against damage or financial loss resulting from a volunteer giving wrong or misleading advice. To avoid liability it must be demonstrated that the museum took reasonable care to ensure that the correct advice was given. But this is open to interpretation. A volunteer acting in good faith can still be liable. This may have particular relevance for volunteers working, for instance, in a financial capacity.

Volunteers are not expected to be experts, but to recognise their limitations and where necessary seek guidance from elsewhere. A disclaimer notice may protect a museum, but the best safeguard is Professional Indemnity insurance. The National Trust will issue a letter releasing volunteers in this position from liability if they are using skills at the request of the Trust for purposes on which they are qualified to advise. They must be in reasonable health, appropriately qualified and with relevant experience for the project.

Personal and Museum Property and Collections

The position of the museum with regard to property lost or damaged by volunteer workers while on duty should be the same as for paid staff. This it is not always stated definitively, as in the government indemnity scheme.

Opinions vary regarding the insurance of museum collections. This has clear implications for volunteers who work with or have access to them. Some organisations view the insurance principle based on replacement as inappropriate to museum collections which are irreplaceable. Some items are replaceable or repairable in the case of damage, however, and many organisations do insure.

National museums and some large local authority museum collections are indemnified by the government and local authorities and therefore are not insured directly. Objects lent by national museums to provincial museums and also between provincial museums are covered by government indemnity.

The usual practice in regard to loans is that responsibility for insurance is left to the lender, if the loan is initiated by them; but if an item is loaned on request from a museum, the museum then insures it and a loan request form is completed containing a clear statement on insurance.

Health and Safety

The Health and Safety at Work Act (1974) states that those who have control of premises have a duty to ensure that they are safe and without risk to the health and safety of all who could be affected by such conditions as far as is reasonably practicable. It is designed to provide a framework for high standards of health and safety at work. A breach of duty can mean prosecution even if no injury is sustained.

The principle underlying current law dates from 1974 when the emphasis on specific duties in the Factories Act was changed to one of general duty. Certain specified activities still come under the Factories Act. They include making, ordering or repairing items in a workshop; but exclude workshop activities in an educational context.

Although the Health and Safety at Work Act applies to employees and members of the general public, duties towards employees are more clearly defined. No categorical statement can be made regarding volunteers, since the terms of the act are open to some interpretation. However, there seems to be a consensus that, in this context, employers should aim to treat paid and volunteer workers alike. An employer could be proven negligent for failing to meet obligations as an occupier of premises by not providing a safe working environment for volunteers in compliance with the spirit and letter of the 1974 Act, even though it does not specifically refer to volunteers.

Employers of more than five people are required to provide a written statement of policy in respect of the health, safety and welfare of employees. The formulation of a Safety Policy starts with a safety audit which lists potential risks. Safety guidelines must then be established and officers appointed to control these risks and provide feedback to managers that duties have been carried out. Feedback is often the missing element in safety policies.

It is advisable to provide volunteers with personal copies of the museum's Safety Policy and to ensure that safety regulations are prominently displayed. Information on potential hazards should be timely and there should be up-to-date information on, and instruction in, the use of insecticides, solvents, electrics and so forth.

Volunteers should be familiar with the Safety Policy of the museum as far as it relates to their area of work. If tools are used, for example, volunteers should not be allowed to use their own. They should be aware of their responsibility to ensure that no action taken by them puts others at risk. It is a supervisor or safety officer's responsibility to provide adequate training and supervision.

Special attention should be given to safety procedures if a person is alone on the museum premises, particularly at 'high risk' sites. Many volunteers work at weekends. Some operate in unattended areas on extensive sites, for example, on restoration projects. The consequences of an accident in such cases could be serious and could devolve to management responsibility although no representative was present. Cases have been reported of some long-standing volunteers flouting newly-introduced rule books sometimes brought in with the recruitment of new, paid staff. Precise job descriptions, careful selection, special safety procedures and skills testing will help reduce risk.

Financial Incentives and Disincentives

Recognition and support for volunteers includes the removal of financial barriers to volunteering and the provision of rewards such as expenses. This ensures that volunteers who give their time and skills free should not, in addition, have to spend their own money. Retired people on fixed incomes and unemployed people generally cannot afford to have their income prejudiced.

Financial questions relating to volunteers first raise the issue of reward and recompense as a principle and, second, bring into focus the need to recognise at which point financial rewards and reimbursement act as a deterrent because they are viewed as notional earnings.

Expenses

The Museum and the Payment of Out-of-Pocket Expenses

The volunteer is important as a component of the museum's staff resources. The best assumption to work from, therefore, is that everyone has a right to claim out-of-pocket expenses. Arrangements for claims and payment should be simple, flexible and fully publicised.

If volunteers do not wish to make a claim they can be encouraged to donate their expenses to the museum. In this case a receipt should be provided so that a realistic picture of running costs is maintained, thus ensuring that no-one is prevented from participating for economic reasons.

Temporarily, the introduction of the payment of expenses may cause some resentment amongst long-standing volunteers who have never before received expenses. The probation service links expenses to an accreditation system, in which only accredited volunteers receive them.

Administrative overheads relating to paid staff are budgeted for but operating expenses in relation to volunteers are rarely considered. This may be a question of omission or collusion. It is good practice to budget for expenses by negotiating or raising funds. If this is not possible, the volunteer should be informed before a placement commences.

The Inland Revenue and Department of Social Security and the Payment of Out-of-Pocket Expenses

The Inland Revenue (IR) and Department of Social Security (DSS) have stated that the reimbursement of expenses to a reasonable level will not threaten benefit or tax liability. This may include travel on a mileage basis (at a rate which is agreed as reasonable and not necessarily the total sum claimed if a large mileage has been incurred); or actual public transport costs. In addition, it may include the cost of subsistence e.g. light refreshments, a main meal and overnight accommodation when necessary.

Payments in cash or in kind in excess of actual costs become earnings. Volunteers should be careful if they are receiving flat rate payments such as daily allowances since these may be treated as revenue by the Inland Revenue and DSS. Actual expenses incurred may also cover telephone calls made from home, car parking and toll fees, special clothing or tools, essential training or events. Advice should be sought. Good record-keeping is essential and receipts are usually required. A monthly claim form should be provided by the museum.

The distinction between 'unpaid' voluntary and 'paid' voluntary work is defined by the DSS leaflet FB26(90). 'Paid' voluntary work involves small payments such as out-of-pocket expenses and a little pocket money. A 'paid' volunteer is treated as a part-time worker. Out-of-pocket expenses paid for travel and subsistence are considered earnings if they exceed the actual earnings disregard. They are then set against benefit or incur tax liability.

Car Mileage Allowances

The law allows a volunteer driver to accept a contribution towards petrol costs, but the problem resides in deciding on fair rates. Unlike the IR the DSS does not define what is an acceptable mileage allowance. Volunteers working for local authorities in social services and, for example, the WRVS, are frequently paid a minimum mileage rate calculated on the basis of a 'casual user' allowance. The rate depends on the car's engine capacity; but the total monthly mileage figure should not exceed an agreed maximum or else travel and subsistence claims are reduced by that amount. There is a great variation in mileage rates and local agreements are often difficult to obtain. Some voluntary organisations work on an agreed, nationally recognised scale. Mileage rates should not leave the volunteer out of pocket.

Current practice frequently does not reflect the principles set down as general guidance above. It is worth trying to adhere to them, however, since cutting volunteer travel expenses below the level of actual costs (which may include a calculation for depreciation) amounts to exploitation. Drivers may be reimbursed without affecting their insurance status and licence class.

'Petrol only' and 'public transport' rates are acceptable for short, infrequent home-to-work type journeys without passengers, but they take no account of the running costs to drivers. Some statutory agencies link mileage rates paid to volunteers to more generous staff rates. There is a strong case for volunteers who cover a large mileage to receive rates that take account of the running costs (based, for example, on figures estimated by the Automobile Association), but excluding road tax and insurance, since these would be incurred in any event. The final sum paid out may be lower than the estimated figures calculated by the Automobile Association but above the amount normally paid.

Lump Sum Payment

When this type of payment is made it often does not cover actual expenditure. However, the volunteer must keep a record of all reimbursable expenses incurred to set against the lump sum, as justified expenses. Any residue will be counted as remuneration.

Honoraria

For tax paying volunteers the honorarium is liable to income tax and the organisation may be required to undertake PAYE responsibilities for it. Expenses for a volunteer's journey to and from work and/or subsistence becomes liable for tax.

Benefits and Entitlements

The DSS leaflet FB26 'Your Benefits, Pension and National Insurance Contributions: Voluntary and Part-time Workers', reissued in October 1988 details amendments for volunteers and those deploying volunteers relating to the 1982 Social Security (Unemployment, Sickness and Invalidity Benefits and Credits) Amendment and Regulations. Local offices work to regulations which maintain the basic principles but amend the rules to make it easier for unemployed people to volunteer.

Unemployment Benefit

Broadly speaking, rules hinge on the volunteer's availability and any payment received. Since March 1988 benefits have not been affected in the following cases:

'Paid' Voluntary Work—Between March 1988 and March 1990 the earnings limit from Monday to Saturday (inclusive) could not exceed £2 on a daily basis. The weekly limit was £43. These figures did not include, for example, free meals, the first 15p of a meal voucher, the first £10 of a Christmas bonus, live-in accommodation and reasonable travel expenses between home and work.

Unpaid Voluntary Work—The 'availability to work' rule gives volunteers 24 hours to relinquish voluntary work in order to attend for interview or take up paid work. Volunteers working in emergencies are exempt; so too, are those attending work camps or giving 14 days a year for charity work. Benefit is untouched if the volunteer is available for work at 24 hours notice and if only reasonable out-of-pocket expenses are received.

At the back of the initial unemployment benefit claim form there is a question asking if the claimant is doing any kind of work. The volunteer must fill in a 'statement of voluntary work' form. This asks about the organisation, type of work, readiness of contact, whether the person is available for interview or to take up a job at 24 hours' notice, and whether s/he is receiving payments. If there are any doubts about availability or payments, other than actual expenses, further related forms will have to be completed and payment of an unemployment benefit will be suspended until a decision is reached. An application for supplementary allowance can be made pending this.

If benefit is disallowed, an appeal can be made to a local tribunal. This may take several months. In successful appeals benefit will be backdated and adjusted for supplementary allowance.

Income Support

Income Support was introduced in April 1988 to replace supplementary benefit. There has been considerable confusion in relation to volunteers since this change. The DSS regulations refer individuals to the Volunteer Centre UK which provides a special form to help volunteers who need to negotiate with local offices about the 'availability for work' rules and to declare expenses claims as legitimate unearned income.

'Paid' voluntary work. If volunteers are unemployed, available for work and do less than 24 hours voluntary work per week it will not necessarily prevent them from getting income support. Payments, however, could affect the amount that they receive. In 1989 the earnings disregard for part-time work, and therefore 'paid' voluntary work, was £5 per week for an individual or £15 for a lone parent. Deductions were made for anything over this. Travel expenses to and from work, however, were also taken into consideration.

Unpaid voluntary work. If a volunteer is unemployed, available for work as above, and receiving only actual expenses, s/he should be allowed support as should a pensioner or single parent. However, if the work is of a kind for which it would be reasonable to expect payment, the DSS will assume that there are earnings from unpaid voluntary work. These are termed notional earnings. Notional earnings are not assumed if the work is for a charitable organisation or of a charitable nature for which no payments are expected or agreed, other than the reimbursement of expenses.

Other Benefits

Industrial Injuries Disablement Benefit and Retirement Pensions present no problems provided that nominal expenses only are paid. For example, retired miners at Chatterley Whitfield Mining Museum receive expenses on a fairly complex scale so that state and Coal Board pension regulations are not contravened.

Invalid Care Allowance ceases in the case of 'paid' voluntary work if more than a certain sum is earned each week. This was £12 in April 1989. If the work is unpaid, the allowance continues unless voluntary activities prevent a volunteer from 'caring' for at least 35 hours a week.

Sickness and invalidity benefits, and severe disablement allowance may be put at risk if volunteer activities are paid or if they raise questions about incapacity. Volunteers must ensure that, if they receive invalidity benefit and severe disablement allowance, they seek their doctor's approval before beginning voluntary work. The DSS must also agree to the work. The maximum that could be earned per week in April 1989 was £28.50.

Maternity allowance ceases for any days on which work is undertaken, paid or unpaid.

Taxation

There have been problems with the taxation of volunteer expenses to and from work. These are treated in the same way as for paid employees who have their expenses met by an employer. The Volunteer Centre UK has recommended the use of the strong argument that, providing there is no contract of employment recognisable in law, there is no obligation on an organisation to prepare a tax return on volunteers at the end of the year. They consider that PAYE regulations do not apply to anything other than paid employment.

Tax is only chargeable on an emolument—defined as a payment (salary, fees, wages, profits etc.)—in return for acting as or being an employee. The payment must be a reward for services rendered. It can be clearly demonstrated that out-of-pocket expenses do not represent a payment of this type. In February 1987, the Inland Revenue sent a letter to the Volunteer Centre UK stating that volunteers are not regarded as being liable in respect of reimbursement of travelling and lunch expenses.

In the United States there are specific tax advantages for volunteers. An estimated value of itemised volunteer time, unreimbursed out-of-pocket expenses and donations to a charitable or qualifying organisation may be deducted on tax returns. At present there are no such incentives to volunteering in the United Kingdom.

III: Working Relations

Partnerships between volunteers and paid staff—or between one group of volunteers and another—planned on an explicit value base are the foundation for successful working relations. Policies, agreements and codes of practice on working relations negotiated by all interested parties to meet the particular requirements of individual museums provide a framework within which good working relations can operate. But, without a positive and active approach to establishing and fostering the right attitudes amongst paid staff towards volunteers, and amongst volunteers towards paid staff, or each other, plans and policies remain inert and ineffectual. Good communications are the key to good working relations in practice.

Everyone in the museum needs to understand why it is important to see working relations between paid staff and volunteers in terms of a partnership. Like paid staff, volunteers are resources and advocates for the museum and its collection. They facilitate the work of the museum whilst increasing the community's understanding and appreciation of that work. Team planning and increasing the visibility of volunteers through, for example, the introduction of badges are ways of developing and acknowledging this partnership. Joint meetings can help paid staff to understand the needs of volunteers, many of whom lack confidence. The isolation of the volunteer often exacerbates this problem and the use of experienced volunteers in a support network for new volunteers can go some way to alleviating the situation. In turn, volunteers need to be made aware of the problems faced by paid staff.

The creation of a post for a volunteer co-ordinator—either in a paid or unpaid capacity—can be of critical importance in establishing and nurturing good working relations. Liaison and communication are major aspects of this job. The volunteer co-ordinator is in a position to encourage team work, demonstrate the value of the volunteer contribution through evaluation techniques and parry hostile or negative attitudes from paid staff. A volunteer handbook or manual can be of further assistance in raising awareness of the position of volunteers as part of the workforce and allay the suspicions of paid staff.

Attitudes of Paid Staff to Volunteers: Problem Areas and Stereotypes

There are many reasons why working relations become strained. Ambiguity and confusion may exist over the museum's long term policies and immediate goals. This can leave paid and unpaid volunteer staff uncertain about the direction and priorities of their own work and the boundaries of their roles. Each side feels threatened by the aspirations of the other and confrontation replaces co-operation.

Too often assumptions are made about staff goodwill without realising that this must be nurtured. Many paid staff find the idea of managing volunteers alongside other members of the workforce distasteful. Volunteers are often 'tolerated' but not involved in the running of the museum. When volunteers are treated as peripheral, they begin to see themselves as second-class citizens whose opinions, knowledge and perceptions have little value.

Paid staff and volunteer rivalry can arise from stereotyped views about the other group. A misunderstanding of motives can be at the root of the problems that lead to poor working relations. It is useful to look at some common negative attitudes of paid staff towards volunteers and their criticisms of volunteer involvement:

Checklist: Stereotyped Attitudes to Volunteers

- Volunteers use up too much time and money.
- Volunteers are not properly trained for jobs and the quality of their work is below standard and inferior to that of paid staff.
- Volunteers are incompetent and lack skills.
- Volunteers are destroying the case for on-going funding.
- Volunteers are taking paid jobs.
- Volunteers are damaging or affecting the terms and conditions of paid workers.
- Volunteers are strike-breakers.
- Volunteers' services are unpredictable and volunteers are not reliable, responsible or accountable.
- Volunteers have a lower level of commitment than paid staff.
- Volunteers are exploited and used as cheap labour.

Note: Conversely some people hold stereotyped attitudes that are more positive in tone but equally misleading: e.g. volunteers are more flexible than paid workers or volunteers are able to achieve results with very few resources.

Attitudes of Paid Staff to Volunteers: Job Substitution and Loss of Funds

The fear that volunteers may threaten jobs and conditions of work for paid staff is the main cause of local Trade Union hostility. This situation can strain relations and curtail volunteer involvement. There have been claims that volunteers affect the terms of employment and conditions of work of paid staff and skim off the most interesting posts. It has been argued, for instance, that volunteers may be given prestige restoration projects or that volunteer guides reduce the number of questions put to paid staff by visitors and, therefore, reduce the level of job satisfaction. On occasions this may happen, but the reverse is also true. Volunteers are often assigned the most monotonous and uninspiring tasks.

The involvement of volunteers is unlikely to be the cause of job loss. Distinctions have to be made between staff displacement and staff replacement. It is unethical for museums to recruit volunteers to save costs. It is also potentially damaging to productive working relations and to the acceptance of volunteers within an organisation. Whilst current difficulties may make this appear a tempting option, legitimate and strong resistance from both trade union organised and unorganised employees can be anticipated. Volunteers themselves would be reluctant to be employed in this way. It is tantamount to exploitation. Moreover, the atmosphere of mistrust and antagonism which is likely to develop as a result of such an action does not make this a desirable move in the long term. All the benefits of collaboration would be lost.

In many museums which have a tradition and backbone of volunteers, or which have no paid staff, these questions will not arise. They may not arise in situations where volunteers are small in number and work on finite projects or clearly defined tasks. In museums where the volunteer input is high, however, it is important to ensure that volunteers are not used for previously paid work. This can be done by negotiation between management and trade unions with the involvement of volunteers. Volunteer policies typically state that volunteers should not do the work of paid staff.

A hard and fast demarcation on job substitution cannot always be applied universally, however, since what is seen as a paid role in one museum is viewed quite differently in another. Moreover, a voluntary job may grow in size and scope to warrant a paid employee.

Professional Standards and Volunteers

Policies and practices for volunteers and paid staff alike should promote accountability and high performance. If high standards in managing volunteers are expected, clearly defined and consistently applied, there will be resultant high levels of performance. Conversely, low expectations will result in low morale and a poor level of performance. Volunteers can, and do, work to high standards.

The challenge for museum paid staff is to ensure that volunteer energies are integrated positively into the functions of the museum as a whole. In order to encourage high standards of performance from volunteers the following points should be considered:

Checklist: Professional Standards and Volunteers

- Remember there is always a cost for quality work, whether it is done by paid or voluntary workers.

- Remember volunteers work best when they are required to meet high but realistic standards.

- Establish volunteer positions that offer reasonable scope for personal and/or professional development.

- Assess the abilities of each volunteer so that s/he can be carefully placed in a job.

- Try to understand the motives of a volunteer in order to find the right incentives.

- Give volunteers clear guidance on the job they are expected to carry out.

- Treat volunteers as peers if they are expected to perform as such alongside paid staff.

- Provide investment in adequate training to enable the achievement of high standards.

- Provide all volunteers with an on-going performance evaluation. This can be used as a development tool.

64

- If a volunteer is not performing effectively in one area, encourage her/him to try a different task.

- Provide recognition for quality performance.

- Ensure strong, effective management, in order not to waste volunteer or staff time.

Volunteer Managers and Paid Staff

Volunteer committees managing other volunteers or paid staff are often working in territory for which they are untrained. Yet their role is extremely responsible and requires considerable skill. Officers may suffer from a lack of confidence because they do not know what is expected of them and staff may suffer from poor management as a result.

Leadership training is an important provision for designated honorary officers. The particular difficulties that they may encounter are limited time to manage and limited knowledge and experience of management. There is also a danger that they may not be fully briefed or be able to maintain regular contact with the staff they are required to manage.

Honorary officers may be ignorant of their obligations towards paid staff, especially if there is no personnel support in the museum. The following points are designed to help in this area of working relations:

Checklist: Volunteer Managers and Paid Staff

- Provision of a statement of terms and conditions within thirteen weeks of an appointment being taken up (good employers provide as far as possible comparable conditions for volunteers as for paid staff).

- Provision of Trade Union Membership.

- Employer's liability insurance is compulsory and the certificate should be publicly displayed.

- Compensation is to be provided if an employee is injured or if there is damage because of employer negligence.

- Provision of a healthy and safe workplace and representation on health, safety and welfare matters.

- The employer or manager has the right to ensure that terms and conditions are being fulfilled and to disciplinary or dismissal measures if not.

- A notice period should be agreed.

- Equal opportunities provision.

- Pay scales should be up-to-date and salaries regularly reviewed.

- It is important to check that holiday entitlements are being taken up.

- A feeling of partnership with staff and clarity of roles should be encouraged to help remove any antagonism. A weekly meeting for information exchange and a discussion of problems and progress is recommended.

- Where practicable and applicable, volunteer managers should accompany staff to training sessions, conferences and outside meetings.

Trade Union Matters

Trade Union membership provides support for and protection to the employee, the possibility of a structured approach to negotiations on terms and conditions of service and an advisory service on a wide range of employment issues. Volunteers often lack this support and access to grievance procedures.

In recent years the influence of Trade Unions on behalf of paid workers within the voluntary sector has spread. This reflects the fact that voluntary organisations have grown in size and complexity and are making attempts to professionalise their structures and services. Employment legislation has become more complex and paid staff in the voluntary sector need expert advice. Most of them cannot turn to personnel officers. In addition, there is concern for job security.

Some national museums have union agreements concerning the appropriate use of volunteers, although these tend to be informal and dictated by custom and practice. Any attempts to monitor the nature and extent of volunteer input appear to be ad hoc. Volunteer activity is generally allowed as long as core jobs are not at issue. The National and Local Government Officers' Union (NALGO) has a policy of guidance to branches on the involvement of volunteers, and there are sometimes local written agreements for museum staff. Independent and university museums are less heavily unionised, if at all.

In 1984 advice was sought from a number of key Unions for the Mattingly Report. These Unions were the Civil Service Union (CSU), representing basic grades of the Civil Service in national museums and galleries; NALGO, drawn from museums and galleries funded by local authorities; the Association of First Division Civil Servants (FDA), representing senior postholders in national museums; the Civil and Public Services Association (CPSA), for secretarial and clerical postholders in national museums and the Institution of Professionals, Managers and Specialists (IPMS), then known as the IPCS, representing specialist grades in the Civil Service, including curators, conservators and scientists in national museums. The unions were generally concerned not to seem obstructive, elitist or discouraging of the enthusiasm of volunteers. The group recommended that negotiations between museum management and volunteers should be followed by a formal written agreement in the form of a code of practice.

The points of concern expressed in 1984 have been reiterated by the unions during research undertaken for this publication. In addition, the National Union of Public Employees (NUPE) and the Transport and General Workers' Union (TGWU) have also been consulted. They all recommend full consultation with interested parties—including management, volunteers and Trade Unions—to establish procedures for good working relations; the need for clear agreement on how, where and when volunteers should be used and the numbers involved; the need for an assurance that neither the jobs nor the career paths of paid staff are placed in jeopardy.

Checklist: Trade Unions

- A formal written agreement on working relations should take the form of a code of practice.

66

- Core functions should be done by paid staff and volunteers restricted to contributing in a supplementary manner. Core functions need careful definition.

- Volunteers should not substitute for full-time paid staff. NALGO have noted an increase in the use of volunteers for work normally done by trained, paid staff.

- Volunteers should not be used to hide staffing shortfalls. This is possible where posts are frozen or there are no new appointments pending restructuring.

- Volunteers undertaking internships or work experience should not be used as a substitute for junior posts.

- Volunteers should not be seen to 'cream off' good jobs and thereby reduce the job satisfaction of permanent staff.

- Volunteers should not increase the risk of accidental damage to the collections. Excess enthusiasm and lack of training or accountability currently characterise many volunteer programmes. This leaves the impression that volunteers are above discipline and regulations.

- Volunteers should not jeopardise the security of collections. Security vetting is deemed necessary. Consideration should be given to who does the vetting—curatorial or administrative staff. This, and the provision and monitoring of keys, are time consuming and rigorous tasks.

- Volunteers should be subject to the same disciplinary procedures as full-time staff.

- During industrial action volunteers should undertake only their normal duties and should not attempt to cross Trade Union picket lines.

- The same standards of performance evaluation applied to paid staff should also be applied to volunteers.

- The appointment of a volunteer co-ordinator is recommended to remove the burden of undertaking ad hoc supervision and training of volunteers from permanent paid staff.

- Volunteer involvement should not put undue pressure on work space and facilities.

A policy document containing a heritage statement was published by the IPMS in September 1989. This Union, which has members in both national and local authority museums, put forward its proposal on the eve of the arts debate at the annual conference of the Trade Union Congress. The document calls for the adoption of a national heritage policy under a single minister. This stance represents a campaign for the maintenance of the highest standards of professionalism and for the adequate funding of core activities. Concern is expressed over the threat to minimum standards in exhibitions, collections and education caused by limited funds. The increased use of volunteers, contract workers, consultants and the appointment of new administrative and commercial staff, such as those in marketing and accountancy at the expense of permanent curatorial and warding staff is not welcomed. Regular use of short-term staff, it is felt, reduces the level of expertise within museums.

The Union is anxious that the number of volunteers and casual staff should be quantified so that the extent of the current reliance on such working methods can be made known. It is concerned that volunteers are inappropriately selected, and that they undermine the jobs of paid staff because of cutbacks in public spending. By implication, in the Union's view, this shows a lack of commitment to our 'national heritage' on the part of the government. As a result, museum management are encouraged to look to volunteers rather than to qualified and experienced permanent staff to meet expanding expectations. The suggestion is that volunteers may lower, not raise standards of professionalism in museums.

Such anxieties are similar to those expressed by Trade Unions in the field of personal and social services in the early 1970s and addressed by the Drain Guidelines. There is evidence, however, that trade union attitudes have become more flexible in these other areas of voluntary activity. In practice, clauses dealing with industrial disputes have been found unnecessarily restrictive because it is impossible to forecast which issues will arise concerning the use of volunteers during the disruption of work of paid staff.

A revised version of these guidelines was issued by the Volunteer Centre UK in 1990 with support from the major Trade Unions and national volunteer organisations in the field of health and social services. The Working Party reviewed procedures in the event of strike action and recommended that where agreement for volunteers to cross picket lines had been reached, documents should be signed by the appropriate authorities in order to avoid embarrassment on all sides. The Working Party also looked at points concerning the extra duties of regular volunteers and those who came forward to help during appeals for emergency public action. Although both these issues have been addressed in the context of health and social services, they have some relevance for museums.

Contingency Planning for Emergency and Industrial Action

Emergency and industrial action may be rare occurrences but it is wise to plan for their eventuality. There follow some recommendations for advance planning, so that spontaneous offers of help from the public can be tapped and used to best effect.

Checklist: Contingency Planning for Emergency and Industrial Action

- Identify the services liable to disruption and the extent to which a reception point would need to be maintained or whether other arrangements, like an answerphone, would be sufficient.

- Nominate an officer to co-ordinate, direct and instruct new volunteers. The officer must be accessible.

- Extra volunteers may be recruited through existing channels, other people or a blanket appeal. Set up a reception procedure.

- The co-ordinator should advise management and interested parties on all aspects of volunteer deployment. Communication channels should be available for passing on essential information, and efforts made to keep them open.

- New volunteers will need a form of induction and, if possible, should be distinguished from regular volunteers.

In the case of industrial action, volunteers should undertake no more voluntary work than normal, or only with the agreement of management and any relevant staff organisations. If volunteers are faced with a picket line hostile to the continuance of their work, they should not attempt to cross it. The situation should be reported to the co-ordinator who should, in turn, discuss it with the unions and management. Volunteers may be issued with a document signed by management and Trade Union representatives indicating the basis on which agreement to work has been achieved.

The appointed co-ordinator should keep in close touch with all volunteers. If services are suddenly forbidden or likely to be upset, this person can explain the circumstances to the volunteers and why there is need for restraint. In the case of the redeployment of regular volunteers, a co-ordinator should obtain the explicit or tacit agreement of the unions. Decisions on whether to do this, when and how, can only be taken at local level. The precise nature of voluntary activities within a museum can be very important in certain situations.

An agreement concerning volunteers drawn up with union officials at the start of a dispute can be advantageous if industrial action escalates. For example, staff may be considered to be working restrictively, and therefore in breach of contract, if they refuse to co-operate with contractors or external volunteers. In this case, they are not entitled to full contractual pay. There may be disciplinary action for breach of normal safety rules and regulations, thereby endangering themselves, colleagues, members of the public and others.

5 | Summary for Action

Policy Planning for Volunteers

'Tailor-made'

A volunteer policy has to be 'tailor-made' to meet the requirements of a particular museum and organised around the potential pool of volunteers in the region. The large number of retired professional people in SE and SW England, for example, makes careful selection both a desirable and a viable option. The sparse population in certain areas of NE England and Scotland means that there must be a greater emphasis on training to maximise the abilities of available volunteers within the community.

'Attractive Package'

The enhanced status of volunteering and demographic trends indicate that there will be increased competition for volunteers in the 1990s. A reduction in the numbers of 16–19 year olds and a 'middle-age bulge' by the year 2000 means that museums will need to offer an attractive package to volunteers if they want to recruit and retain good people.

'Reciprocity'

Volunteering is based on the principle of reciprocity. Volunteers do not come free. People's motives for volunteering in the museum sector are many and various. The chance to pursue a special interest or hobby, meet like-minded people, stave off loneliness, use their expertise, offer a service to the community, add to their own knowledge in a life-long education or begin a career in the museum field are just some of the factors that motivate people to volunteer. Each has a personal agenda. In return, volunteers expect a high degree of satisfaction, respect for their contribution, and working conditions commensurate with those of paid staff. Commitment is required from both the volunteer and the museum.

'Consultation'

The planning process involves a review of the existing volunteer resources and a new policy may necessitate changes in the way volunteers are deployed. Consultation gives coherence to the formulation of volunteer policy and eases its implementation, whilst maintaining the ethos of volunteer activity. Some or all of the following participants should be included—volunteers, paid staff, the volunteer organiser, trade union representatives and members of the Friends Association.

'Core' Functions

The identification of 'core' functions is important in those museums where volunteers work alongside paid staff. The Museums Association's *Policy Statement of Volunteers in Museums* emphasises that the value of volunteers is in a supplementary and supportive role. Only in exceptional cases, it states, can volunteers replace the trained, qualified permanent staff in the museum. The expansion of recognised museum functions to include the care of visitors as well as the care of collections has led to a wider range of 'core' activities. Twelve are highlighted by The Museum Training Institute. Each museum must decide, for example, whether guiding and information services—often traditionally provided by volunteers—should be considered part of 'core' or support functions. In the area of conservation, clear distinctions need to be made between preventive conservation tasks suitable for volunteers, including NADFAS Volunteers, from work requiring the expertise of a conservator.

'Supervision'

Volunteers take time to supervise. A volunteer co-ordinator, either on a paid or unpaid basis, can increase the visibility and acceptability of volunteers amongst paid staff and ensure the smooth running of a volunteer programme. S/he can negotiate job descriptions with curators/managers, instigate recruitment schemes, arrange rotas, keep records and, when necessary, start disciplinary proceedings. If a curator/manager is responsible for the supervision of volunteer tasks on a day-to-day basis, this should be included in her/his job description.

'Communications'

Good communications are fundamental if fragmentation of the volunteer effort—and a consequent reduction in its effectiveness—is to be avoided. A co-ordinator can produce a newsletter, offer a friendly word and liaise with Friends Associations. Joint meetings between volunteer and paid staff can be arranged. The provision of a general common room for tea and coffee establishes informal lines of communication.

'Resources'

In addition to staff supervision time, other physical and financial resources are required to operate a successful volunteer programme. Space to work and the right equipment are important. So too, is providing insurance cover (including, employer's and public liability, personal accident, vehicle and professional indemnity), paying expenses and offering training. The increase in administration is unavoidable. Some Friends Associations operate on an independent basis within the museum; but this has the disadvantage of removing them—psychologically at least—from the main management structure. What is a cost-effective return on investment in volunteers? Volunteer hours need to be converted into a monetary equivalent to find the answer. How many volunteers a museum needs on either a project or long term basis can only be assessed once areas of work and individual tasks for volunteers have been identified in relation to the corporate plan.

'Procedures'

A loose-leaf manual detailing recruitment, induction and training procedures and giving information on such matters as insurance cover, the payment of expenses, discount at the museum shop and codes of practice on Health and Safety, for example, offers a practical reference guide for paid staff and volunteers alike. It assists the integration of volunteers within the management framework on the museum as a whole. Copies of the volunteer agreement, job descriptions and information on the Friends Association are useful additions. A statement on the volunteer policy, history and current management structure of the museum can also be included.

'Review'

There is a need for a regular review of the relationship between volunteers and the museum. A mechanism for this should be built into any volunteer policy. Volunteers offer a museum flexibility and a chance to pilot new schemes at low cost. They can fund raise to provide new acquisitions, give their time to help disabled visitors and bridge the gap between the museum and the community through informal contact and formal public relations activities. Some volunteers are themselves disabled, some are oral history sources in their own right. Many have an infectious enthusiasm that can be wearisome for paid staff. Careful planning and good management can ensure that this keen energy adds an extra dimension to the quality of the museum service and is channelled to meet a museum's immediate objectives and long term goals.

Appendices

Appendix I

Sample of National, Local Authority and Independent Museums to Compare Management Practices and the Involvement of Volunteers in Different Museum Functions

Name of Museum/Gallery	Mersey Maritime	The Tate Gallery	Victoria and Albert	RAF	GAGM	Godalming	Peterborough
Status	N	N	N	N	LA	LA	LA
Paid staff	c	c	c	c	c	b	b
Volunteer Organiser	*			*	*		
Number of volunteers	200	65	115	50	170	40	20
Friends/Supporters	2000	*	4000	3000	2800	190	
Volunteer Activity							
a) Management							
b) Curatorship							
c) Education						*	
d) Guiding	*	*	*	*	*		
e) Documentation		*		*		*	*
f) Conservation	*		*				*
g) Research				*			
h) Information	*		*			*	
i) Fund Raising	*		*	*			
j) Security						*	
k) Clerical							
l) Other				1		2	3
Management Practices							
a) Recruitment	*	*	*		*	*	
b) Induction	*			*		*	
c) Training	*	*	*	*	*	*	
d) Evaluation	*	*	*	*			
Time Commitment							
a) Rota		*	*		*	*	*
b) Flexible		*	*	*	*	*	*
Incentives/Rewards	1					2	3
Other Relevant Information					1	2	3

Horsham	Bodleian	Whitworth	Ashmolean	Beamish Open Air	Chiltern Open Air	MSI	National Tramway	American Bath	Severn Valley	Vale and Downland
LA	U	U	U	I	I	I	I	I	I	LA/I
a	c	c	c	c	b	c	c	b		a
	*	*	*	*		*	*		*	
29	30	25	20	*	150	100	375	100	400	100
215		1100		*	1100	600	1500		15000	120

Horsham	Bodleian	Whitworth	Ashmolean	Beamish Open Air	Chiltern Open Air	MSI	National Tramway	American Bath	Severn Valley	Vale and Downland
					*				*	*
					*					
		*			*	*		*		*
*	*		*	*	*	*	*	*	*	*
*		*		*	*	*				*
*				*	*	*	*		*	
*				*	*	*	*			*
*		*		*	*	*			*	
		*		*	*	*	*		*	*
					*					*
*		*	*	*	*	*				
		4	5	6		7			8	9

Horsham	Bodleian	Whitworth	Ashmolean	Beamish Open Air	Chiltern Open Air	MSI	National Tramway	American Bath	Severn Valley	Vale and Downland
*		*	*		*	*	*	*	*	
*					*	*	*	*		
*	*				*	*	*	*	*	

Horsham	Bodleian	Whitworth	Ashmolean	Beamish Open Air	Chiltern Open Air	MSI	National Tramway	American Bath	Severn Valley	Vale and Downland
*	*	*			*			*	*	*
	*	*				*	*		*	*
4	5	6	7		8	9		10	11	
4	5		6		7					8

Key

Other Volunteer Activities

1 Publicity caravan, organising annual lecture programme.

2 Running the Local Studies Reference Library.

3 Exhibition work.

4 An outreach programme for the disabled, elderly, infirm and visually-handicapped.

5 Handling sessions for visually-handicapped children.

6 Costumed volunteers responsible to the newly-appointed Keeper of Interpretation.

7 'Project Planet'—building a full-size replica of Stephenson's steam locomotive.

8 Operation of the railway—drivers, firemen, signalmen, guards, travelling ticket inspectors, booking-office clerks and station masters. Publicity, marketing, sales and catering outlets, painting, cleaning and gardening.

9 Catering.

Incentives and Rewards

1 Star ratings and badges for each team.

2 Honorary membership of Friends Group. Newsletter.

3 One volunteer was nominated by the Curator for an Award in Amateur Palaeontology from the Palaeontological Association.

4 Payment of expenses. Bouquets are sent to volunteers on their birthdays. A cookery book, bottle of wine and catering course were provided for one volunteer who cooks for functions at the museum. Free parking, invitations to functions, press coverage of volunteer work and lots of 'thank yous'.

5 Travel expenses.

6 Expenses claimed at 10p per mile. Cup of tea. Own room.

7 Payment £3.00 per hour "Semi-volunteers".

8 Friends free entry to the museum, end of season party, newsletter.

9 A 'Volunteer of the Year' award is given.

10 'Semi-volunteers'—payment £3.90—long afternoon. Own room. Newsletter and free refreshments.

11 Reduced fare travel. Quarterly magazine

Other Relevant Information

1 Language skills are required for The Burrell Collection. Trade union acceptance of volunteer guides despite high unemployment in the area.

2 Procedures Guide.

3 Contract for volunteers—see Case Study 6.

4 Basic Guide to Museum Fund Raising. A stand at an 'over 50s' day run by the Leisure and Recreation Department: attracted 2 new volunteers.

5 Guidelines have been prepared by Library staff so that tours do not disturb readers.

6 The low budget is supplemented by the dynamism of the Volunteer Organiser. Charge for service.

7 Wardens' Information Pack. Paid staff are chosen for their likely ability to be accepted by volunteers. Information dissemination is a problem.

8 Guidelines—Notes for keepers. Short shifts for elderly volunteers. Entry in the Egon Ronay Good Food Guide.

Appendix II   Case Studies

1. Victoria and Albert Museum, London—National
2. The Whitworth Art Gallery, Manchester—University
3. The Museum of Science and Industry, Manchester—Independent
4. The National Tramway Museum, Crich, Derbyshire—Independent
5. The Cookworthy Museum, Kingsbridge, Devon—Indpendent
6. Peterborough Museum, Peterborough—Local Authority
7. Ruddington Village Museum, Nottinghamshire—Independent
8. The Smithsonian Institution, Washington DC,—National
9. Boston Museum of Science—Independent

The following case studies are examples of good practice. They have been selected because the management, or self-management, of volunteers is of a high standard and appropriate to the management structure and goals of the organisation.

Case Study 1

The Victoria and Albert Museum

At the Victoria and Albert Museum volunteer support is long established. There is a large Friends organisation with over 4,000 members and a group of active Friends have operated the information desk for over seven years. More recently, a programme of guiding under the direct supervision of the museum has been successfully introduced. There is also a programme for student internships.

Information Desk

Visitors to The Victoria and Albert Museum need help in finding their way around the building; finding out what there is to see in the galleries and where particular exhibits are to be found. A rota of 60–70 Friends work on the Information Desk on the basis of three shifts a day. They are organised by a member of the public affairs staff who provides up-to-date information and oversees training.

Recruitment is not a problem. Volunteers are mostly women who live in close proximity to the museum and they include American, Dutch, German, Russian and French people based in London with their husbands for a short time. Their language skills are useful. No expenses are paid. Volunteers have quarterly meetings with speakers from the Museum staff. At Christmas they receive a diary and have drinks with the Director. The main reward, however, is enjoyment in the work.

Guides

The Museum introduced a guiding programme in 1988 and implemented the full programme in 1989. Volunteers were considered the best means of delivering this new service on a number of counts. The scheme was designed to improve community relations, stimulate interest in and access to the collection and to be cost-effective. It was felt that only volunteers were available in sufficient numbers to offer the freshness needed of a guided tour and, at the same time, be cost-effective. A system of paid guides would cost in the region of £50–100,000 and lack the enthusiasm, individuality and local contact offered by volunteers.

The guides are organised by a member of the education staff and recruitment is both from the Friends organisation and elsewhere. Prospective volunteers are interviewed and are required to have an interest in art history rather than formal qualifications in the subject. There is an age limit of seventy and each guide must agree to undertake at least forty tours a year. All thirty guides—both men and women—serve in turn on the Guides Committee.

Introductory tours are offered as well as thematic tours on British Art and Design. Special needs are catered for: there are tours for groups with disabilities, tours in a second language—French, Spanish or Italian—and special family tours in the school holidays for those with children in the age range 7—13 when two guides are used. Groups can book a premier tour which includes refreshments and a souvenir pack. A £3 donation is recommended.

Training is rigorous and is undertaken by the Education Department and curators. Guides have to pass a three months introductory course before they can work with the public. A staff advisory panel monitors the tours to ensure that high standards are established and maintained. Each guide gives two tours a day, every two weeks and is encouraged to undertake research in the library, attend a monthly seminar and the public lecture programme. Guidelines are provided for those individuals who choose to work with visitors who are visually impaired. Each guide receives a newsletter every 3 months. This includes details of new books, comments from the public and provides a mechanism for self-evaluation. One guide quoted a visitor's remarks: 'Today an American lady with her daughter told me she had been to the museum last year on a specialised guided tour and had enjoyed it so much that she came again this year with her daughter'.

Guides have a clearly defined role within the organisation and are expected to offer a high level of commitment in return. They are not paid expenses. Tea and coffee provided by the Friends free of charge are available in the volunteer/study room. Volunteers wear a badge, which according to the information sheet is 'to protect them from being asked by members of the public to take more responsibility than they should'. Over 18,000 visitors took advantage of the scheme during its first year of operation.

Internships

Internships are provided on a formal basis in the Conservation Department and a number of student placements are arranged in the National Art Library and curatorial Collections. Guidelines are available for those seeking one of the ten places in the Conservation Department. Recruits are selected by a Board in February to start the following September for a period of between six months to one year. In order to be considered an applicant must have completed a recognised training course in conservation or have been working in a relevant discipline in a recognised institute for three to four years. No payment is offered but neither is there a charge for workspace.

Junior internships of at least a month are available in some of the curatorial Collections. Students who are considering a career in museums and who have completed at least two years of their degree course can apply by letter directly to the Curator of the preferred Collection. Applicants are considered in March or April for a place during the long summer vacation. Selection is by interview. No expenses or other remuneration are paid. These internships are regarded as a form of work experience and students are supervised to do the kind of work typically undertaken by permanent staff.

Short term placements for students following postgraduate vocational training courses are also available. Students from the Ealing School of Librarianship undertake placements of two to six weeks in the Library. In the Prints, Drawings and Paintings Section a student working on the postgraduate programme run jointly by the Museum and the Royal College of Art gave valuable assistance on the Crazy Cat Archive.

Case Study 2

The Whitworth Art Gallery

'Our reward is the pleasure we get from the privilege of working in a friendly and exciting gallery'.

The Friends organisation at The Whitworth Art Gallery with over 1,100 members operates in close association with the Director and staff of the gallery. A kitchen, now turned into a bistro, is shared by both. The main focus of the Friends' activities has been in the field of fund-raising and public relations. Friends have run the library at the Gallery for many years and are responsible for cataloguing all incoming publications. Two volunteers also operate a joint programme with staff for disabled and elderly people on a visits and outreach basis.

Fund-raising and Public Relations

The Friends have recently raised £40,000 in eighteen months as their contribution to an appeal launched by the University for an extension to the main gallery so that a large part of the wallpaper and textile collections are accessible to the public in 'open stores'. This will also allow room for changing exhibitions of prints and drawings. Funds raised by the Friends have helped to maintain high standards in terms of acquisitions in the face of high sale room prices. Support for publications has also been given. Centenary Year, 1989, was promoted by three cards marketed by the Friends illustrating items in the collection. Other events included a 'silent auction'.

The Outreach Programme

This scheme started as an experimental student project with the elderly in the galleries. Friends took it over to provide continuity and it has now become tailored to special needs. The programme is carried out in close association with gallery staff and is designed to meet the needs of disabled, elderly, infirm and visually-handicapped residents of retirement homes, day centres and occupational therapy departments of hospitals. There is a need for one-to-one contact and the programme involves a rota of some thirty volunteers. Objects and textiles from the collections form the basis of reminiscence sessions at targeted homes. After this visitors come to an open day at the gallery. They are greeted by Friends, who show them round the Gallery, have tea and cakes and are given a gift pack to take home. The work was publicised in a directory of community-based projects after it was featured in a series 'It's My City' on BBC television. There is no charge for the service. The modest costs are met out of the Friends' funds; the volunteers report that they find the 'work' especially rewarding.

Organisation

The main Friends committee meets three or four times a year and plans a series of social events, outings and behind-the scenes tours of the Gallery for new Friends. The Tuesday Team organises the 'active' wing of the Friends. The Chairman, Honorary Secretary, Honorary Treasurer, Programme Secretary, Membership Secretary, Volunteer Organiser and Publicity and Outreach Organiser meet in the Friends Room. They arrange behind-the-scenes help for the gallery including filling envelopes for mailings. They operate a catalogue table at major temporary exhibitions, for which the Gallery offers expenses at the rate of ten pence per mile. Other costs associated with operating the Friends Association are covered by the Friends funds. They have their own room and 'consider themselves very lucky'.

Case Study 3

The Museum of Science and Industry, Manchester

Voluntary activity at The Museum of Science and Industry in Manchester is organised through the Friends of the Museum. It has over 600 members. During any one week up to 60 volunteers will be working at the museum. Many are retired and offer a wide range of skills and interests. The museum gives them a warm welcome and they work in close association with paid staff in a supportive role. Clear policy decisions have been taken to ensure that they do not undertake core functions and good procedures ensure easy working relations with paid staff. Volunteers are fundamental to the museum's growth, the quality of its projects and the excitement of its interpretation. In turn, volunteering at the museum serves an important social function within the community.

Volunteer Tasks

Volunteers undertake a wide range of tasks and without their help it would be difficult to operate train rides at weekends, maintain a high standard of presentation in the Air and Space Gallery and pioneer new projects. For example, the current 'Planet Project' and planned new exhibitions that will attract women as well as men. The range of tasks includes:-

- Operating steam train rides at weekends

- Track maintenance, restoration and refurbishment of locomotives—training provided

- Demonstrating the printing press

- Assisting in the engineering workshop under the supervision of workshop staff to the specifications of curatorial staff

- Cleaning exhibits in the Air and Space Gallery: each volunteer identifies with an aircraft and operates according to procedures set out by curatorial and workshop staff

- Clearing tables in 'Tracks' restaurant at weekends

- Guide/interpreters of the 1830s station complex

- Taking a stand to promote the museum at shows, steam fairs and the Castlefield Carnival

- Writing and editing the Friends newsletter with assistance from the public relations staff

- The Planet Project

Student Placements

- Assisting in the design studio—six to eight weeks: Manchester Polytechnic and Blackpool College of Art

- Assisting manager/curators: including two French management/language students and Leicester University Museum Diploma students

The Planet Project

A team of volunteers is building a replica of Robert Stephenson's steam locomotive 'Planet'. This was originally built for the Liverpool and Manchester Railway in 1830. The project is run completely by volunteers, including technical and fund-raising committees, in consultation with the Director on strategic decisions and in close liaison with the Workshop Manager. Full-time staff assist this team effort with help in pattern-making and the machining of components. Ground rules laid down in advance ensure smooth working relations. A marketing strategy is being worked out by the Director, marketing staff, Chairman of the Friends and sponsors prior to the unveiling. A video is being made about the project and the BBC programme 'Blue Peter' is planning a special programme on it.

Organisation

The policy to include volunteers in the management structure of the museum in a supportive role, provide clear procedures on volunteer tasks and the implementation of both through careful supervision is the key to the success of the Friends' involvement at the Museum. A Volunteer Co-ordinator is appointed through REACH—the Retired Executives Action Clearing House—and job descriptions for paid staff include the supervision and assistance of volunteers where this is appropriate. By organising volunteer support through the Friends, insurance is guaranteed. The Friends have charitable status and undertake their own secretarial and financial affairs. A 'Volunteer of the Year' award is given. Nominees are chosen by a panel made up of the Director, Friends Chairman and Volunteer Co-ordinator.

Case Study 4

The National Tramway Museum, Crich, Derbyshire

The National Tramway Museum was started by volunteer enthusiasts and experts in the 1950s. Although a core of paid staff have been working there since the 1970s, it remains a volunteer-led organisation with a democratic system of management. The Tramway Museum Society is a registered charity and was incorporated as a company limited by guarantee in 1962. The Board of

Management is the formal policy-making body. Members of the Board, who are also Directors under the Companies Act, are all volunteers and are elected at the Annual General Meeting. Each Board member has a specific reporting function covering at least one of the Museum's activities and some have direct executive responsibility. Monthly meetings are also attended by the paid Manager and the Curatorial Adviser.

Collection policy was determined at an early stage according to criteria approved by members in a general meeting following recommendations by a committee of members. This still forms the basis of the collection although the policy has been reviewed on two occasions by a reconstituted committee and minor modifications have been made.

One meeting for members held in 1989 was a self-evaluation of what is meant by effective (and enjoyable) membership. It looked at standards and training meeds. The first generation of retired workers with the appropriate engineering skills is dying out. Who replaces them and who has the enthusiasm to continue the work are serious questions that are being addressed by a number of industrial and transport museums with a high level of volunteer involvement.

The museum is an example of an area of specialist interest where people are prepared to work hard to preserve and restore trams in working order and build up a reservoir of specialist knowledge. Although there is a core of five permanent staff in the workshop, in addition to the manager and other paid staff—including a librarian and some seasonal staff—control of the museum remains with the Managing Board and the responsibility for its future remains with the membership who vote for them.

Organisation

The manager—formerly employed as an engineer in the steel industry—sees his role as a facilitator who co-ordinates activities, ensures that there are smooth communications and markets the product.

The current membership of the Tramway Museum Society is over 1,500 and around 25% of the members give 'hands-on' help. Two houses on the site provide accommodation for members from all parts of the country to work at the museum. Volunteer Co-ordinators take over from the manager at weekends although he is sometimes required to work on Sundays. This stipulation is included in his job description. There are no formal interview or monitoring procedures for new volunteer recruits. High standards are maintained through careful supervision. Volunteer work is divided into two main areas—the workshop and operating the tram service. A third area of activity involves volunteers with specialist knowledge.

The Workshop

Volunteers contribute to tram restoration and maintenance in the workshop mainly at weekends and paid staff work there during the week. A rigid division, however, is not possible, neither is it seen as desirable. The allocation of duties by the 'Volunteer Leader'—paid or unpaid—depends on available skills and commercial or operational demand. Safety is a key issue and the running fleet is checked routinely. Challenging and complex tasks are combined with mundane jobs like rust scraping. Some volunteers are extremely skilled.

The Tram Service

The tram service is operated virtually entirely by volunteers. It runs every ten minutes along a mile of track. Volunteers start as conductors and are then eligible to train as drivers if they are available on a regular basis. Training is arduous since no two tramcars are alike. A separate driving test and licence is issued for each of the different categories of tramcars. The chief instructor, who is a chaplain, attracts publicity through his unusual hobby.

Drivers and conductors also talk to visitors about the museum and sell them 'riding' certificates which help to fund the restoration work. At the end of the day they are responsible for cleaning out the tram and reporting any defects to the workshop. The Museum takes very seriously its responsibilities to the public in operating safely. Standard fire and health and safety procedures are strictly adhered to. The high voltage used in running the tramcars has implications relating to public liability. Construction and operating procedures are discussed with the Railway Inspectorate as required.

Specialist Advice

The Museum probably has more knowledge about tramways amongst its members than any other museum in the world. The 'hands-on' experience which the Museum has gathered in over 30 years' development at Crich has provided it with a unique practical expertise in the maintenance, conservation, reconstruction and operation of historic tramcars and the construction and maintenance of the track on which they run. This advice is in demand from other museums such as The North of England Open Air Museum, Beamish, Co. Durham. The Museum's library, largely created by volunteer effort, has a unique collection of books, films and photographs. The ability of the Museum to offer consultancy services, however, is limited by the immediate pressure of the day-to-day demands of running the Museum.

Case Study 5

The Cookworthy Museum, Kingsbridge, Devon

The dynamism and success of this museum is due to a highly-developed management structure for volunteers. This includes a volunteer handbook, in-house manual for stewards and 'mini-manuals' for the curatorial team. When the consultant part-time curator was asked what the volunteers do, the reply was: "Virtually everything. They run the Museum with curatorial guidance from me (2 days a week). The only thing we do not do is conservation with the exception of basic treatment to farm machinery".

Volunteer Committees, Teams and Activities

There are 140 volunteers, mostly retired in-comers to the area, out of a total membership of 400 in the Museum's Society. Approximately 100 act as stewards undertaking ticketing, sales and wardening duties on a rota basis. These are organised by the one paid member of staff, the Warden. There are ten members of the Management Committee with special administrative responsibilities including marketing, insurance and organising leases; ten members of a curatorial team who are responsible for looking after the costume, photographic and machinery collections as well as accessioning and documentation, local history research and education. There are also ten craft instructors. The accessioning and documentation are being computerised and a catalogue is in the process of preparation. One volunteer who undertakes research is putting local family history records onto a database. Those people most interested in artefacts tend to be the ones who work in a curatorial team and those who are most interested in people do the stewarding.

Organisation

Recruitment, induction and training are of major importance. There is a waiting list so volunteers are carefully selected and then trusted. Induction sessions for new stewards are also used to update long-standing volunteers in any changes and new procedures. The curatorial team is recruited from the ranks of the stewards. If someone wants to move to that team s/he does one year as a relief steward. Space is at a premium and the co-ordination of the days when volunteers are in the Museum working is as critical to the smooth running of the operation as good communications. Despite an excellent handbook, a manual for wardens and mini-manuals for the curatorial team there remains the difficulty in maintaining communications and circulating relevant information amongst 100 stewards who work on a rota basis sometimes at weekly or fortnightly intervals.

Manuals

The consultant curator, Kathy Tanner, produced a handbook: *Museums Projects. A Handbook for Volunteers, Work Experience and Temporary Staff,* which was published by the Area Museum Council for the South West with the help of an Office of Arts and Libraries grant. This handbook covers three basic areas of volunteer involvement—display, documentation and education—and gives a general background to the Museum's work as well as details on the tasks that are allocated to volunteers. Initially, the idea of the handbook was to provide continuity in a museum with only part-time paid professional help. However, it has become a source of help and inspiration for other museums. The stewards' manual is updated regularly and is designed to assist stewards in facing any eventuality. It includes information on fire and emergency procedures, what to do if someone offers a donation or money, how to deal with wheelchairs, what information to give in the form of a 'potted history' and finally the answers to common questions.

What this organisational structure achieves is a confident, self-assured volunteer team. As the Honorary Secretary comments, "Discipline is not a problem and is largely achieved by exhortation and reassurance; there is a good team spirit". Some volunteers come for "something to do to keep the mind alive" and there can be a problem if a minor physical disability, for example visual impairment, becomes worse and the Museum is a life line for social reasons. The family atmosphere is genuinely that for older volunteers and visitors alike. Two thirds of the volunteers are women. One person trained in Museum Studies in the USA. All volunteers are regarded by the insurers as employees and are covered under Employer Liability Insurance. The optimism is created on a firm foundation and the Museum is able to operate to a high standard at 'rock bottom cost,' according to one of its members, because of good organisation, good procedures and the immense amount of time given by volunteers.

Case Study 6

Peterborough Museum

Welcome to Peterborough Museum. We are grateful to you for offering us your services and we look forward to having you working with us. Every volunteer has his or her special contribution to make to the Museum, and we will try to help you realise yours.

We at the Museum recognise the vital role played by volunteers. In particular, we know that without your help it would be quite impossible to manage all the Museum's varied collections.

The following guidelines have been prepared with a view to helping you become familiar with Museum routines, both for your protection and for the well-being of our collections.

Extract from: *A Contract for Volunteers Working at Peterborough Museum*

This straightforward introductory welcome to Peterborough Museum by the Curator of Museum Services sets the right tone. Although a prospective volunteer discovers on page two of the contract that expenses cannot be paid, the next point reminds the individual to ask the Curator about careers in the Museum Service. The contract also details attendance requirements, supervision requirements gives information on equipment and how to use it and insurance cover. Each volunteer is asked to sign this agreement before commencing work.

Organisation

The five full-time curatorial staff are doubled by a regular group of five volunteers out of a total of between fifteen to twenty. They work at set times in project groups undertaking such tasks as cataloguing photographs, ceramics, paper and manuscripts and undertaking basic documentation and conservation work with close supervision. Volunteers deal only in preventive conservation—keeping collections stable, for example, through environmental control systems. The onus, however, is on documentation—a Museum Documentation Association system is used. This area of work has top priority and has resulted in a successful application for registration. There is no Friends Group.

Working Relations—paid staff and volunteers

Museum staff view making facilities available for volunteers who want to work with the collection as part of their professional services. These cover Social History, Archeology, Fine and Decorative Art, but there is a bias towards Geology and Natural History. One retired volunteer, a former science teacher, became interested in geology. In 1990 he was awarded the Palaeontological Association's first Award for Amateur Palaeontologists largely on the strength of the work he has done at the Museum. Another young volunteer has subsequently done a degree in Geology. Volunteers are a mixture of local retirees, unemployed people, students and NADFAS Conservation Volunteers who were prominent in helping the Museum in the 1970s.

There is a clear distinction between the tasks undertaken by paid staff and those carried out by volunteers. Volunteers do not do guiding. Curatorial staff do this on an ad hoc basis. Volunteers have a major input during the preparation for an exhibition. In fact, it would be impossible to hold many of these without the blocks of time put in by volunteers. Alternatively, contractors would have to be used and that would be prohibitively expensive. One volunteer prepared a natural history diorama and others helped to put together a touring exhibition on children's art. A graduate in history and archaeology on a Work Experience Programme assembled the Museum's nursery display. Schoolchildren sometimes come for a three week placement in connection with Project Trident and then return as volunteers in the sixth form.

Case Study 7

Ruddington Village Museum, Nottinghamshire

For over twenty years volunteers have run Ruddington Village Museum through the Executive Committee of Ruddington Local History and Amenity Society. This all-volunteer museum is based at two sites in the village: The Hermitage and St Peter's Rooms. Displays in the first focus on material from archaeological excavations undertaken by members of the Society and the domestic lives of Ruddington people and, in the other, they concentrate on the community life of the village and include an Edwardian fish and chip shop, pharmacy, ironmonger's cobbler's shop and school room. The Museum has been granted full registration under the Museum Registration Scheme.

The Management Committee is responsible for planning and decisions concerning the accession, disposal and conservation of artefacts. Led by the Hon. Museums Officer thirty four active volunteers work on all the tasks associated with running a small museum from security, cleaning, maintenance and clerical duties to research, conservation, documentation, exhibition design, guiding and attracting new recruits. The Hon. Museums Officer comments: "Only very occasionally are jobs felt to be beyond the scope of volunteers, usually because they are potentially dangerous or require specialist equipment". There is emphasis on training and the newly-appointed Volunteer Co-ordinator is responsible for this as well as recruitment and appraisal. The informal organisational structure with loose-knit teams is matched by an informal approach to appraisal. This is done mainly by observation.

Research is considered a key strength in the Museum and involves around twenty volunteers. Both individual and group research is undertaken for publications and for temporary exhibitions. No charge is made for family history research and for GCSE projects but voluntary donations are often made by appreciative recipients. Visitor care includes explaining the archaeological excavations that have taken place and answering queries as well as general guiding duties.

Conservation is taken extremely seriously and a great deal of volunteer input goes into the inspection and ongoing conservation of artefacts on display and in store. The Hon. Museums Officer comments: "Difficult conservation tasks bring out the best in suitable volunteers, but we depend on professional advice and discreet supervision".

Over a six month period the Museum had access to advice from the East Midlands Area Museums Service's (EMAMS) Conservation Consultant and thereafter supervision was continued by the Museums Officer. These demonstrations combined with the pooling of knowledge and attendance at in-service courses means that the conservation team is a group of skilled people who are increasingly gaining in experience. Delicate or complex tasks are earmarked for special attention by a paid conservator. Tasks that are undertaken include protecting metal items from corrosion, the lubrication and greasing of items with moving parts, the treatment of wooden items for woodworm, polishing, varnishing and painting and the repair and care of textiles and dolls from the toy collection.

The Chip Shop Project captures the magic and excitement of establishing and working in a small community-based museum. It also shows the professional approach of the Society. It is described here by the Hon. Museums Officer:-

"An old man died in the village in 1985 and an Edwardian fish and chip shop was rumoured to exist on his premises. Volunteers were involved in what became known as 'The Chip Shop Project'—from the investigation of the rumour through to the reconstruction of this remarkable find in the Museum.

First, volunteers contacted the Executor and arranged to view the place. They found the old fish and chip shop locked up since 1941 when the owner (the son of the couple who had originally opened it in 1902) went off to war, leaving it exactly as it was when it was last used, with the fat in the frying pans and the ashes in the fire box of the coal-fired range. They decided to accept the fish and chip shop in its entirety from the Executor.

The group then consulted the Area Museums Service for advice and grant aid. They photographed, measured and made a scale plan of the exhibit as it had been found. They cleared away debris (including the congealed fat), dismantled the range, potato peeler and other large items and transported the whole collection to the Museum. The conservation team took expert advice and undertook training in the techniques they required. They ordered the special conservation materials that were recommended, cleaned the artefacts and carried out the appropriate conservation measures. This took twelve volunteers six months to complete. When the equipment was reassembled every item was accessioned, indexed and catalogued. Then the setting was reconstructed to the plan that had been drawn before the removal of the exhibit from its original location.

Meanwhile, volunteers researched the development of the fried fish trade, contacted the Fish Fryers' Federation and the manufacturers of the equipment. Some handled the publicity and immense media interest, wrote articles and appeared on television and local radio. Finally, they arranged a formal opening, invited guests, made speeches and entertained those who had accepted. This is our most spectacular exhibit and volunteers constantly tell the story to visitors and answer their questions about it.'

Case Study 8

The Smithsonian Institution

The Smithsonian Institution more than double their paid staff by employing volunteers—some 5,252 in 1989. There is an impressive management structure for volunteer programmes organised by the Director of the Visitor Information and Associates Reception Center. A leaflet on *Opportunities for Volunteer Service* is given to prospective volunteers. Apart from information desk volunteers and individual departmental programmes, there is a focus on docents (guides) and behind-the-scenes volunteering.

The Director, Co-ordinator of Docent Programs at the National Museum of Natural History and Chief Officer of Education Programs at the National Museum of American Art and the Manager of the Behind-the-Scenes Volunteer Program are women. The last three have all been volunteers. This experience has provided them with an awareness of and sensitivity to the issues that arise when employing and managing volunteers. One commented: "If you've got to err, you've got to err on the side of generosity or leniency and if you don't have that worked out you're going to lose 300 of them. So if you can't give them a little leniency and overlook little things, then you shouldn't be in the position you're in." There is a delicate balance between recognising the needs of the volunteer and establishing formal procedures to ensure the accountability of the volunteer to the Museum. At The Smithsonian Institution this balance is achieved through a combination of clearly defined procedures published in handbooks and the careful selection of managers as well as the careful selection of volunteers.

Behind the Scenes Volunteer Program
Opportunities available, Fall 1989.

Areas of Work:
Bibliographical preparation, collections management, cataloguing, record-keeping, filing, indexing, research and general office work.

Subjects:
Translation Services, Aviation, Photo Archives, History of Art, Administrative and Curatorial Units of most Departments, Library.

Manager—Behind the Scenes Volunteer Program'

sensitivity
negotiator
make jobs interesting'

Volunteer

- *Letter to prospective volunteer* outlining current opportunities

- *Volunteer Registration Form* completed includes: special skills, education and spoken and written language abilities (used for records and administrative purposes)

- *Short Term Special Projects Inventory Form* (completed) Gives details of people/skills available when prompt action is need for one day—1 week

- *Personal Interview*
  — discuss project
  — referred to supervision
  — work agreed by volunteer

Staff

- *Volunteer Project Description* completed includes: numbers of volunteers required, special skills, level of education, dates and names of supervisor and time keeper

- *Guidelines for Short Term Special Projects*

- *Project Supervisor*
  — discusses with volunteer
  — work agreed by supervisor

Provisional Period
"test the waters" 1–3 months

- *Handbook* provides background training and establishes standards—includes *Roles and Responsibilities* of volunteer and supervisor and *procedures,* attendance requirements, insurance and termination

- *On the job training* provided and formal commitment as laid out in the handbook expected

- dismissal possible

Problems:
Handled by the manager according to procedures outlined in the Handbook

Termination of Project
letter of thanks
evaluation form completed by volunteer

Evaluation form sent to supervisor

Records Maintained
Information from Registration and Evaluation forms accessed onto a computer database

Time Sheets filled out and returned to BVP programme office monthly

+"If you want someone just to type all day that's boring, boring—you need to enrich the project, make it more meaningful and make someone want to stay for a long time.'

Manager, Behind-the-Scenes Volunteer Program, December 1989.

Docent Programmes

The National Museum of American Art

The Chief Officer of Education Programs organises 80 volunteers who work with both adults and children as well as running occasional children's workshops, family festival days and giving tours at special exhibitions. Five have been working at the Museum since its opening twenty two years ago. Since Washington is a transient capital, this is something of an achievement.

Volunteers are mainly women—mothers with young children—and increasingly, retired professional people. They work one day a week. Initial training sessions are carried out only every three or four years because there is a low rate of attrition. A Board including a Chairperson, Treasurer, Secretary, Program Secretary and individuals responsible for adult liaison and school liaison and a trip organiser, assist with interview procedures. This process is highly selective. Advertising is done directly on local radio, television and in local newspapers. Students are not encouraged to apply. The museum is seeking commitment over a number of years.

Training is rigorous—two days a week for six months, four hours a day. New docents learn about the administration and conservation aspects of the Museum and they are given talks on American Art History by each of the curators in turn. Reading lists are supplied. A 'dialogue approach' is taken to guiding and training is given by matching the talk in the morning on, for example, nineteenth century colonial portraiture with training in techniques in the afternoon. Individuals are taught how to raise visitors' curiosity through question and answer methods, how to construct a tour, keep the thread going and, at the same time, limit it to one hour. At the end of the six months they are tested by giving a 'mock tour' to a group of their own friends. If this is not satisfactory it is repeated. The organiser considers, however, that the highly selective interview process ensures that there are very few unsuitable docents and that 'failure' is not a problem.

Incentives for volunteers include a visits programme to other museums and sometimes to Europe, free catalogues, free tea and coffee and a 20% discount in the book store. The importance of maintaining a chain of command and lines of accountability is stressed by the organiser. 'Oh there's no question about it, they (volunteers) are unpaid staff in this Museum. They know the curators when they see them in the hall but there's a fine line there. While they may know them or say hello to them, any requests to see them come through me. This is the same as for paid staff. Everyone knows her or his place'.

The National Museum of Natural History

Three hundred volunteers work at this Museum and recruitment takes place every year. The thematic programme is mainly orientated to schools but there are some adult tours. 28,000 hours were given by volunteers in 1989. The pool of available people and recruitment methods are similar to those of the National Museum of American Art, although docents have to be invited back each year. The programme is particularly attractive to mothers with young children since it is organised around the school year.

The training period for new docents is long and arduous—seven half days a week for seven weeks with four additional half days to learn teaching techniques, as well as time to follow three different experienced docents. In this way docents acquire a grasp of the subject matter in conjunction with the methodology. There is an emphasis on concepts rather than 'a thousand little trivial facts', even with very young children of kindergarten age. Here one concept is offered to 'tie things on'.

Scripts are available for each of the different tours but docents are required to absorb the material in order that there is a lively interaction with the visiting groups. Baskets of 'touch-its' bought from a biological supply house, and occasionally given by the curatorial staff who can be somewhat 'miserly with them,' offer a tactile dimension. The updating of both new and established docents in the latest finds and scientific thinking is considered important to enable them to be 'good teachers'. Training is given once a month between November and May.

The partnership between the Museum and volunteers is emphasised by the Chairperson of the Docent Committee working side by side with the Co-ordinator of Docent Programs in her office. Although the volunteers have no legal right to prepare guidelines or bye-laws themselves, it is considered a moral right as long as all decisions are taken in consultation with the Co-ordinator who remains the line manager.

Case Study 9

Boston Museum of Science

The range of voluntary activities at this Museum are designed to appeal to different age groups with a variety of educational and social backgrounds and encourage those in full-time work to give a short-term commitment to the Museum. Out of almost 1000 volunteers approximately half will be active in any one month. In 1989 volunteers gave over 76,000 hours to the Museum, representing an equivalent of 46 full-time employees. The Volunteer Services Unit is like a Personnel Office for volunteers. It co-ordinates services and ensures consistency in terms of job descriptions and the handing out of benefits, maintains standards and accesses details about volunteers, hours of work and programmes onto a computer database.

Staff and volunteers work together and volunteers take on where the staff leave off, maintaining a fine dividing line. There are exceptions. The scanning electron microscope is operated by volunteers who, unlike staff, use them at work. The diversity and drive of volunteers at this Museum is impressive. The group it finds hardest to attract are middle-aged, middle-class housewives—the traditional volunteer. The search for people who are able to offer a long-term commitment, in addition to those who volunteer on a short term basis for individual projects, is seen as a major challenge for the 1990s.

Special Exhibitions

Docents and interpreters are trained for temporary exhibitions. Many people do not want a 'lifetime' commitment. Once the exhibition is over they are able to re-negotiate their contract, or not. This means they are able to accommodate volunteering around family and career and chose to work on exhibitions that interest them. Involvement is limited to between three to four months on a regular weekly basis. *Trapped in Time: Treasures of the Tar Pits* (1989) about the La Brea Tar Pits, California, appealed to those interested in Ice Age fossils.

Discovery Centres

Volunteers work in partnership with paid staff on educational programmes. One volunteer, Jim, has been coming to the Museum three to four days for ten years since he retired. He has been awarded various pins and badges but said: "I never wear them. They mean nothing to me. I love working with children". He was talking to a fourth grade class about reflection. In contrast, Marie—working in the Human Body Discovery Space—displayed all her pins for 150 hours, 500 hours, 1,000 and 2,000 hours. She used to work at the Massachusetts Institute of Technology and commented 'We are walking exhibits—I have had two cataracts removed and another volunteer has had two hip replacements. We can say to the children—look!'

Science by Mail

The volunteers working in this programme are 'real scientists'—doctors, engineers and a professor of physics from the Massachusetts Institute of Technology. There was an overwhelming response from an advertisement in the newsletter for The American Association for the Advancement of Science and the Museum now has a list of 350 experts. Children pay a fee and receive three question packets a year with three problems to solve e.g. waste disposal at a Space Station. Each child receives a direct reply from a 'mentor'. The volunteer has an open-ended option and the child has an opportunity to make contact with top scientists. The co-ordinators of the scheme at the Museum screen scientists to ensure that they are not judgmental. One child psychologist was quietly dropped from the list.

Pre-school and Parents

This scheme is designed to show parents, and particularly mothers, how to respond positively to science. The programme has been extremely successful and has been worked out with the education department. The course is either four morning sessions or four Sunday mornings. It is limited to 6 parents. After three years of development the scheme is ready to be handed over to a paid co-ordinator.

Inventors Week-end

This Trade Show for amateur inventors was started by volunteers and receives 18,000 visitors over a period of three days. Its success has meant that it is now worth paying someone to operate this and the volunteer input has been withdrawn now that the development phase is complete.

Function Sales Unit—Star Parties and Dinosaur Parties

This scheme is both popular and profitable. Three requests a week are received for birthday parties at the Museum. It is a strictly fund-raising activity and restricted to members only. They pay $100 and $10 for each child. The Star Party includes exclusive use of the Planetarium and there is also a less popular Dinosaur theme. Women volunteers organise these parties which always make a profit of $100.

Appendix III Volunteer Organisations and Support Services

Volunteer Organisations

United Kingdom

The tradition of supporters groups in museums in the United Kingdom has been well established for over a century. It is only in the last twenty years, however, that national volunteer organisations have been set up in response to the rapid growth of community involvement in museums, the expansion of their numbers, and development of their work. The British Association of Friends of Museums (BAFM) was formed in 1972 and the National Association of Decorative and Fine Arts Societies (NADFAS) was founded in 1968 with its active wing—the Voluntary Conservation Corp (VCC) added in 1973. This is now called NADFAS Volunteers (NVs). Duplication of effort has been avoided in the United Kingdom by the establishment of the Heritage Co-ordination Group to which both BAFM and NADFAS belong.

Italy

Just over ten years ago the Voluntari Associati Per I Musei Italiani (VAMI) was founded in Milan, Italy. The purpose of setting up a new organisation was to encourage people to give their time and expertise and so go beyond the fund-raising activities of Friends' groups. The emphasis is on guiding and research. Training is a major concern as it is for NADFAS Volunteers. However, VAMI is not involved in conservation work.

North America

Specialist organisations in North America include The Volunteer Committees of Art Museums of the United States and Canada (VCAM). This meets every three years and is planning more frequent regional meetings. Issues relating to guiding are the focus of interest of the National Docent Association in the United States. Their attention is currently directed towards helping the 'crisis in the education system' and encouraging learning outside the classroom through the use of volunteer guides. The American Association of Museum Volunteers (AAMV), on the one hand, like BAFM and NADFAS has a composite role and is concerned both with promoting high standards of volunteering and opportunities for the educational enrichment of its members through workshops and discussion groups.

The British Association of Friends of Museums (BAFM)

BAFM was founded almost twenty years ago with the aim of uniting museum Friends throughout the country and helping them to support their museums more effectively. The Association provides members with a means of exchanging ideas and combining to advance the cause of museums and galleries to the government, the public and the press. Friends see themselves as advocates of paid professional staff.

Apart from a campaigning role designed to achieve greater recognition and financial support for museums, the Association offers members a wider forum for social gatherings and educational activities including lectures and tours. Advice is available on approaches to fund-raising and public relations. Insurance is available for Friends who become actively involved in the day-to-day work of the Museum.

The Association is run by a council whose members represent groups in the regions, corresponding approximately to those covered by the Area Museums Council. Over 216 member groups representing approximately 150,000 individuals receive a year book, a regular broadsheet and the news-sheet of The World Federation of Friends of Museums. The broadsheet is also sent to groups abroad.

BAFM presents an award for the most interesting and best-presented newsletter. In 1989, this was given to the Friends of The Black Country Museum, Dudley.

Two publications much in demand are *How to Start a Friends Group* (1986) and *Are You Insured?* (1990).

The current priorities of BAFM are to strengthen international links through The World Federation of Friends in Museums; encourage a broad-based membership, especially the recruitment of young people through a youth membership scheme, and to give more financial support and more help in terms of time to museums.

Setting up a Friends Group

The essential elements are careful planning, close liaison and consultation with museum staff and regular communications. Alongside BAFM's guide on *How to Start a Friends Group,* the following points should be taken into consideration.

Consultation on the constitution: Friends and museum staff

Provision for a Friends' committee member to be on the Board of Trustees (where applicable)

The designation of a representative of the museum staff to sit on the Friends' committee as an ex-officio member

The appointment of a volunteer co-ordinator in large Friends organisations e.g. Mersey Maritime Museum

The production of a handbook including administrative information, names and addresses of committee members, a calendar of dates, details of projects

The provision of office accommodation or a base in smaller museums

The creation of banking facilities

The setting up of regular review procedures—possibly every five years

Affiliation to BAFM

The National Association of Decorative and Fine Arts Societies: Volunteer Groups

NADFAS was founded over twenty years ago to increase the enjoyment, knowledge and care of the arts and to stimulate interest in the preservation of the cultural heritage. Affiliated Societies organise lectures, study day, outings and tours. Members undertake to do voluntary work for a range of heritage organisations including museums, historic houses, The National Trust and libraries.

Approximately 60,000 members in over 250 autonomous Societies in the UK pay fees to the parent Association, governed by a national Chairman and Executive Committee with sub-committees controlling various aspects of its activities. Societies are growing rapidly and there are waiting lists for membership. Twenty affiliated Societies are located elsewhere in Europe and in Australia.

About five to ten per cent of the NADFAS membership actively volunteer. In 1973 the Volunteer Section was formed and an organised system and training procedures were established. Each Society (DFAS) Chairman is provided with written guidance on starting up a volunteer section if one does not exist in an area. New groups are discouraged from actively volunteering in their first year. As a result, NADFAS workers have a reputation for a professional attitude, dedication and reliability combined with the ability to work well with established staff

The Nature of the Work

NADFAS Volunteers do not conserve as such but do preventive conservation 'housekeeping' and are honest about the limits of their abilities. Groups enjoy good working relations with the Conservation Departments at the National Maritime Museum, The National Trust and with the United Kingdom Institute for Conservation (UKIC).

92

Volunteers dust and dress books but do not repair them; they check and care for textiles but do not restore them. The scope of the tasks is increasing all the time. Amongst the variety of skills offered by NADFAS members are the cleaning and refurbishment of books, ceramics, silver, arms, armour, furniture and textiles; library work and paper conservation; the indexing, cataloguing and recording of church contents, vernacular buildings and trees in historic gardens; the making of replica furnishings and costumes; research and translation; administration and accounts; guiding and stewarding.

Finding a role for amateurs in the field of conservation becomes more difficult as conservation becomes more specialised. The training needs of NADFAS Volunteers are emphasised within the Association through the funding by the society of study days and in-house training provision for special projects. This attention to training in specific skills recognises the sensitive nature of conservation work.

An Education Committee has been set up recently to take over the running of study days and introductory courses and provide further opportunities for all NADFAS members. More day and weekend sessions are planned at places such as West Dean College, Chichester. Training in inventory work is being developed with the Museum Documentation Association (MDA). The new Museums Training Institute (MTI) is working closely with NADFAS to develop further training for volunteers in preventive conservation work.

NADFAS: Volunteer Procedures

A formal Joint Agreement on Volunteer Procedures is currently being developed into a Handbook. The aim is to provide information for group leaders and prospective employers on NADFAS working methods—including an emphasis on education and training, close co-operation with conservators and reporting and evaluation techniques. A brief outline is given here:-

1. Starter Pack
NV Group Leaders copy and circulate this to members. It includes:
  Introduction to volunteer work
  NADFAS Insurance policy
  List of NV representatives in UK
  Programme of NV Study Days and other training
  Specialist Information on starting a Library Conservation Project
  Forms for formalising and regulating procedures

2. Preparatory Visit
NV Group Leader visits the museum/property to discuss the tasks with the director/curator/owner.
  the project is identified
  description and estimate forms are completed including
  number of volunteers required
  roster proposals
  estimated expenses and arrangements to meet them
  Report and forms sent to NV Chairman for approval

3. Checks
Group Leader investigates and checks the following:
  working conditions
  — conforming with Health and Safety
  — refreshment break
  Accessibility of staff
  Provision of materials
  Reimbursement of expenses
  Registration of record and indemnity forms completed in triplicate and signed by the employer,
NB Indemnity for NADFAS is against third party claims at work

4. Selection and Training
Group Leaders aim to choose the right people and ensure the right training is given before a project begins.
  Skills register of NADFAS members (gradually being computerised)
  Training 'in situ' or through Study Days—funded by NADFAS
  Advice from AMCs and specialist consultants e.g. Textile Conservation Centre Hampton Court and National Trust Library consultant.
  Punctuality and reliability are emphasised.

Volontari Associati per I Musei Italiani (VAMI)

Italy is the European country with the greatest number and variety of works of art, archaeological remains and monuments. Yet there are immense problems. Cultural institutions lack the staff to supervise volunteers or space for them to work and they cannot provide training. Italy does not have a tradition of volunteering in this sphere and there has been considerable opposition to volunteers, even in more traditional roles. A breakthrough has only been achieved through the foresight, persistence and successful results of the Association of Volunteers in Italian Museums (VAMI) and the encouragement of several enlightened museum Directors.

This, the only national association of museum volunteers in Italy, was founded in Milan in 1978. It aims to promote the cultural heritage through the practical help of volunteers. It mediates with the public and private sectors; helps safeguard Italy's artistic-historic heritage by publicising problems which are not receiving urgent solutions and organises emergency help when public provision is lacking. In fact the Association came into being as a result of the Milan Friends responding to the appeal for help from the Castello Sforzesco and the Poldi Pezzoli Museum.

VAMI is largely self-financing and develops its work through pilot projects planned in co-operation with paid professional staff. It now has groups based throughout Italy including Florence, Lucca, Messina, Naples, Prato, Reggio Calabria, Varese, Venice and Verona.

VAMI directs its work from a central headquarters based in part of the Poldi Pezzoli museum. The parameters of voluntary service are fixed for each programme in discussion with curators and museum managers. There is also liaison with public bodies to ensure community needs are met. This collaboration is considered important in view of the sensitivity on the question of volunteering in Italy. As a result, problems with unions and paid professionals are rarely med. Projects are always new and innovative and the emphasis tends to be on guiding and research. In some museums volunteers only provide school tours while paid professionals provide adult tours. VAMI does not help with conservation work as this is considered to be a highly specialised and delicate area. This initial resistance means that nothing has been done without careful research, structured systems, hard training, and practice as VAMI could not afford to make mistakes and needed to build credibility.

VAMI: Procedures

Recruitment

Information Desks at Exhibitions
Two interviews:
(i) Exchange of information/creation of records (the form requires two referees)/skills and interests.
(ii) Matching a volunteer to a workshop.
    Handing out documentation.

Induction

A pack includes information on the background and structure of VAMI, details of other groups, and international conference papers, as well as insurance cover.

Training

Self-preparation—selecting study materials relevant to a project and developing a work plan, attending seminars. Weekly meetings with the Study Advisor 'Consulente Didattico/a' and Group Leader.

Testing by two questionnaires—if successful, VAMI membership.

Work Groups

Leader and Study Advisor—limited in size: group psychology considered important.

Handicapped in the Museum Group (1981)	*Research Group* (1981)
Guided tours for the disabled in Milan Cathedral. Emphasis on access and *enjoyment* of the collection. Monthly visits for blind or partially-sighted. Allowed to touch statues. Architectural fragments chosen by the Curator and Psychologist. Braille plan.	Private art collection in Milan. Data prepared for computer classification in libraries. Training: international conference in Pisa on the Processing and Automation of Art History Data and Documents (1984).

Church Cataloguing Group (1985)
Request from Archbishopric. Cataloguing
works of art, photographing and writing a
report on churches in the diocese.

Junior Group
Educational guiding. Immense potential. Art
education is compulsory but underfunded,
VAMI works with teachers following models in
USA and UK. *But* VAMI guides not Art Historians—cannot take a 'disciplined' approach
as the Tate Gallery.

Secretariat Group
Indexing, filing, correspondence, bookings and
a press cutting service. Administrative support
for other groups. Accounting. Press liaison.

International Group
VAMI hosted an international conference in
Prato in May 1989 on The Role of Cultural Volunteers in Heritage Organisations. Trans-
lations, attendance at international conferences,
links with France, Switzerland and UK.

Cultural Hostesses
Reception, information and guiding services.
Special exhibitions only. Training: Art History
Milan University. Colour coding.

White Hostesses Messina Museum
Welcome, transcribing and distributing monthly lectures by art experts. Use of dramatic
techniques in guiding to show the history of
Milan through sculpture—'mini play' each
guide takes one of 6 parts.

Red Hostesses
Gallery of Modern Art in the City Villa Belgioso
services tailored to needs of public in consultation with museum management, town council
and other organisations. Important exhibitions.
Paid guides also work there.

The Association of American Museum Volunteers (AAMV)

The centrality of volunteer activity to American Museums and the incorporation of voluntarism
into the American way of life means that volunteers are integrated into the museum community.
Volunteer schemes are largely organised by museum staff many of whom are women, and were
once volunteers themselves.

As a result of the different approach to volunteering in the United States and with the direction
of volunteer activity frequently in the hands of museum managers, the volunteer organisations
associated with museums have a different, and somewhat lower profile than they do in Europe.
Ladies' committees such as the one attached to Boston Museum of Fine Art act in an autonomous
capacity both within the museum and within the United States.

The AAMV alone represents volunteers in all categories of museums. Membership is over
110,000. It aims to promote professional standards in volunteering and provide a forum for the
exchange of ideas and information at home and abroad in co-operation with the WFFM. It publi-
cises projects and programmes locally and nationally to volunteers and volunteer managers. Opportunities for members to undertake continuing education through discussion groups and workshops
are also a primary concern. The Association works in close co-operation with museum directors,
staff and Boards of Trustees. Like BAFM—the nearest UK equivalent—members belong to the
WFFM.

Organisation

The genuine difficulty of maintaining communication between members across such a wide geographical area and within a wide variety of museums without an administrative base is acknowledged. The annual meeting of the AAMV in May 1989 addressed the question of the Association's
general decline. The President commented, "This has been a year of assessment for this organisation,
assessment which has resulted in the realization that this organisation can be viable, productive
and organized". There are now plans to establish a staff position in Washington. A new membership
leaflet has just been produced.

A newsletter is published twice a year.

A Directory of Museum Volunteer Programs was published in 1988 by the Association of American Museum Volunteers. Information is based on a national survey of over 700 museums. It is the first publication in the United States about voluntary services to museums and there are plans to update it. The Directory is of special value to co-ordinators of volunteer programmes and lists the number of volunteers in each institution, what work they are involved in, contact names and numbers, the type of organisation and programme. Indexes of geographical listings by state and city encourage volunteers and volunteer managers to become familiar with colleagues and resources in their own area.

A Handbook for Museum Volunteer Programs, is planned. The first of its type, in the United States, is intended as a 'hands-on' reference manual with information on setting up and developing various types of voluntary programmes.

How To Be A Happy Volunteer
A Bill of Rights for Volunteers
1. You should know, before you agree to work or volunteer the time, day, length of tour, etc.
2. You should have been provided a job description that adequately and completely describes the duties and responsibilities of your job and explains to whom you are responsible.
3. You should know how and under what conditions you will be evaluated and what the consequences of the evaluation will be.
4. You should know if there is a "career ladder" for your job and what rungs you must climb.
5. You should be treated with dignity and respect by other volunteers and by staff. Each of you brings a richness of experience and intellect and skills to your position and you should be able to utilize these life experiences without threatening anyone or their positions.
6. You should have the ability to discuss problems or anxieties with the person in charge. You should be able to do this without fear of repercussions and with a feeling that these problems will be considered.
7. If you decide that you do not like your volunteer job you should be able to discuss the reasons with the person in charge. You should also know that there may or may not be other opportunities for you within the museum.
8. You should receive consideration for another volunteer opportunity if at all possible.
9. You should receive some reward for the work that you do. If you are doing this purely for the reward, you are there for the wrong reason.
10. Finally, you should feel good about the volunteer work that you are doing and the contribution you are making to the museum and to your community.
© Created by American Association of Museum Volunteers—Texas, U.S.A.

How to Have a Happy Volunteer
1. You should explain, before the volunteer begins work, the day, time, length of service, special circumstances etc. There should be no surprises.
2. The volunteer should be provided with a job description stating the duties, responsibilities and to whom the volunteer is responsible.
3. The volunteer should know if evaluation is part of the job. They need to know who will be evaluating, how often, under what circumstances and the consequences of that evaluation. Is there a possibility of promotion, demotion, reprimand? Is the evaluation for self improvement purposes? Is it to improve the training program?
4. You should tell the volunteer if there is a "career ladder" for the job and what rungs must be climbed for certain rewards.
5. You should be prepared to treat all volunteers with dignity and respect and encourage volunteers to treat each other with respect. Volunteers bring with them a richness of experience, intellect and skills to their position and should be able to utilize these life experiences.
6. Volunteers should feel comfortable discussing problems or anxieties with the person in charge. They should be able to do this without fear of repercussions and with the feeling that what they have to say is being given fair consideration.
7. Volunteers should be able to decide that they do not like the job they have been assigned. They should be able to discuss this with the person in charge and be considered for an alternative position, providing one is available, within the volunteer structure.
8. Volunteers should understand that, as representatives of an institution, they have an obligation to uphold the policies and regulations of that institution and they may be asked to separate themselves from the institution if they fail to meet the criteria for their job.
9. Volunteers have no right to expect rewards for what they do but most volunteers function better with carrots instead of sticks. Staff should try to enhance the volunteer's self image; remember to say thank you and never ask a volunteer to do something that she wouldn't do.
10. Finally, you should feel good about the volunteer work being done in your institution and the contribution that your volunteers make to the museum and their communities.

Support Services

The experience, expertise and resources available from The Volunteer Centre UK (VC) and the National Council for Voluntary Organisations (NCVO) although directed principally toward social action are of significance to those volunteering or managing volunteers in museums. The basic difference between the work of the NCVO and The Volunteer Centre UK is that the former concerns itself with back-up to voluntary organisations in England, whereas the latter focuses on the volunteer and how organisations work with them in the UK. In the 1990s voluntary organisations will face major challenges and more than ever need to be clear about the roles they should be taking. These two national organisations are equipped to offer help and support.

The Volunteer Centre UK

The Volunteer Centre UK promotes volunteering in the community and acts as an advisory, research and resource centre. It was set up in 1973 to assist voluntary organisations, small groups and individuals who work with volunteers to develop good practice in the involvement of volunteers.

The Centre offers a comprehensive service. This includes the provision of up-to-date information about employer responsibilities in relation to volunteers; advice on the design and delivery of training aimed at developing skills in the management of volunteers and access to recent information and current research on a wide range of issues concerning volunteers through an on-line computerised data-base (VOLNET UK) and publications programme.

The Centre co-ordinates UK Volunteers Week each year (June 1–7 in 1991) which provides an opportunity for museums to promote their volunteers' work or to express appreciation for their involvement.

National and International Role

The Centre convenes the UK Volunteering Forum comprising a cross UK membership of key volunteering organisations. It has also initiated a European network of national volunteer centres, and in 1988 produced, together with other participants, the first-ever World Charter on volunteers.

Publications

These include the following:-

Volunteers—a journal published 10 times a year

Good Practice Guides—booklets on topics such as Recruitment, Expenses, Evaluation and Relations with Local Authorities

Resource Packs—For example on 'The Tax and Notional Earning Position of Volunteers', 'So you want to be a Volunteer?'

Handbooks and training packs

Guidelines defining areas of work, legal structures and seeking support from the business community

Catalogue—a free booklet describing all the Centre's services and products

Voluntary Action Research Papers—A series of research papers relating to volunteering themes including motivation of volunteers, the costs of volunteering, local government contracts and their effect on volunteers. A major national survey of volunteering will be published in late 1991.

The National Council for Voluntary Organisations (NCVO)

Established in 1928 as an independent charity, the NCVO protects the interests and independence of voluntary organisations and promotes policies, actions and new projects to tackle social problems. With similar Councils in Scotland, Wales and Northern Ireland it forms the UK National Councils for Voluntary Organisations. The NCVO is the main resource, representative and development agency for the English voluntary sector.

The NCVO works towards creating the right conditions for effective voluntary action through legal and statutory back-up and the provision of practical information. A bridge is built between voluntary organisations, central and local government and the private sector. The organisation played a leading role in the introduction and implementation of the Charities Act, 1960, which extended the scope of the Charity Commission. The membership of over 800 organisations ranges from small groups to large national bodies. As the owner of the Bedford Square Press, it publishes over 70 books and reports on the voluntary sector each year.

There is a need to improve public and political recognition of and support for the role of voluntary organisations. An annual voluntary sector lobby meeting at the Houses of Parliament is co-ordinated by the NCVO. For instance, it sponsored an amendment, later supported by the House of Lords, to allow charities 80% rate relief under the Community Charge system. This concession is worth £55 million to charities.

A study group, the Policy Analysis Unit identifies major trends, examines working relations in a changing environment and acts for high standards in fundraising, training of trustees, management and general conduct. It is involved in long-term consideration of the implications of new legislation on the voluntary sector.

Local Development and Action

The Council attempts to provide structure, technical and training back-up to Local Development Agencies, forge partnerships and set up new projects to strengthen effectiveness. Current areas of local voluntary action include community care, self-help, management training, urban regeneration in Action for Cities, housing, Equal Opportunities issues, inner city and rural decline, provision for ethnic minorities and employment initiatives.

In 1987 the NCVO formed a new Rural Unit to promote and support voluntary action in rural areas and ensure the sensitivity of the policies of statutory and private agencies and the appropriateness of NCVO's projects and services to rural circumstances. The Organisation Development Unit was set up to support groups like black and ethnic minorities in voluntary sector development, especially where traditional funding sources have declined.

Information and Advice

The Library and Information Unit circulates information through its information sheets and publications. A range of management, personnel, legal information and advice is provided. Topics covered include charity law, fundraising, education, race relations, guidance notes and specimen constitutions.

The National Organisations' Management Unit (NOMU) was launched in 1987, with the aim of helping voluntary organisations to work with trainers and consultants and to be more effective in management development without losing their values and objectives. It holds Management Forums.

The NCVO Personnel Unit receives requests about staffing problems, job evaluation, recruitment and introducing Equal Opportunities policies.

Citizens Advice Notes Service (CANS). These provide a comprehensive digest of social and industrial legislation e.g. a series on the Social Security Act.

NCVO News is published ten times a year and is free to members. It provides information concerning policy developments, management education, relevant views and information and notice of events, seminars and training courses.

Practical handbooks include a *Voluntary Agencies Directory*.

Bulletins to update voluntary organisations on current issues e.g. *Contracting: In or Out?* are sent free to those on a mailing list.

Appendix IV Suggested Guidelines for The New Volunteer

It is in the interests of management and the museum that the volunteer should be fully informed and aware from the start. The volunteer will also reap the rewards of the increased effectiveness, satisfaction and confidence that information will bring.

The following guidelines are offered with this in mind:

1. Ensure that you know exactly what is expected of you, the nature of your task, and what respective roles are with paid staff, whether this is written down or not. A job description which clarifies commitment and responsibility is preferable.

2. It is important to agree the extent of your commitment, which should be definite but should not over-commit you. Offer only as much time as you can give regularly. Reliability is important.

3. Make sure that you know to whom you are accountable, who is responsible for support and advice and how they are accessible before you being work.

4. If you are unable to keep to agreed arrangements, it is essential to inform your supervisor.

5. Know who to contact in an emergency or other special circumstances.

6. Be prepared to work within the limits agreed with your supervisor. If you feel there is any form of change needed, discuss it before taking action.

7. Remember that work is undertaken by agreement. You may decline any suggested task if you wish and you have a right to propose a change.

8. You have the right to know that work you are doing is not depriving anyone of paid work.

9. Familiarise yourself with Health and Safety arrangements and any other special procedures. Establish what to do if something goes wrong. Satisfy yourself that your working environment is adequate and find out whether recreational facilities exist.

10. Check insurance cover and who insures. Insurance should be extended to include all volunteers, who should be covered for injury during the course of work and provided with at least public liability insurance.

11. Check and position on reimbursement of expenses incurred during work. You should be encouraged to claim them.

12. If you need to learn new skills, training should be provided.

13. Find out whether there will be periodic evaluation and how your skills and work will be evaluated.

14. Make sure that you understand where your contribution fits in. There should be an adequate induction and instruction period at the beginning giving you background to the organisation, introduction to staff and management, to the work and workplace, and instruction in using equipment or machinery.

15. Apart from doing your job, you will be expected to maintain the same principles of management and discipline laid down for paid employees.

16. Once involved, opportunities should be provided for you to meet other volunteers and members of staff for mutual support and information exchange. You may be invited to attend team or staff meetings periodically.

17. You should have a right to feel that you belong and to contribute. You should feel free to express views and opinions through recognised channels. You should have access to decision-making processes such as representation on the management committee.

18. You need to establish the procedure to follow if you have a grievance or complaint. If you are

unable to establish a friendly relationship with anyone you work with or feel that you are not making progress, inform your supervisor and discuss the matter.

19. If, for whatever reason, you decide that you want to leave, provide an explanation and reasonable notice, if this is possible.

20. Your volunteer service may be more satisfying if you relate it to other work in the field. Discuss with your supervisor the best way to develop your knowledge. You may be expected or invited to attend any relevant in-service training schemes or outside courses and conferences. Check where further training is available and whether it will be provided to you free.

21. Be prepared to give an evaluation of the volunteer programme from time to time and upon leaving. Guidelines for this are provided later in this section. Comments and suggestions are welcome at any time.

Select Bibliography

American Association of Museums, *Managing Volunteers for Results*, Public Management Institute, American Association of Museums, 1979.

Adirondack, Sandy, *'Just About Managing'*, London Voluntary Service Council, 1989.

Fletcher Brown, Kathleen, *The Nine Keys to Successful Volunteer Programs*, The Taft Group, Washington DC 20016, 1987.

Grinder, Alison L. and McCoy, E. Sue, *The Good Guide: A Sourcebook for Interpreters, Docents and Tour Guides*, Ironwood Publishing, Scottsdale, Arizona, 2989 (5th edit.), 1985.

Handy, Charles, *Understanding Voluntary Organizations*, Penguin, 1988.

Holloway, Christine and Otto, Shirley, *Getting Organised—A Handbook for Non-statutory Organisations*, Bedford Square Press, 1985.

Mattingly, Jenny, *Volunteers in Museums and Galleries*, Volunteer Centre UK, 1984.

Museums and Galleries Commission, *Guidelines for a Registration Scheme for Museums in the UK*, HMSO, March 1989.

Pearson, Anne, *Arts for Everyone: Guidance on Provision for Disabled People*, Carnegie UK Trust and CEH, Dunfermline and London, 1985.

Prince, David R. and Higgins-McLoughlin, B., *Museums UK*, Museums Association 1987.

Tanner, Kathy, *Museum Projects: A Handbook for Volunteers, Work Experience and Temporary Staff*, The Area Museum Council for the South West, 1988.

Wilson, David and Butler, Richard, *Managing in Voluntary and Non-profit Organisations*, Routledge, 1989.

Wilson, Marlene, *The Effective Management of Volunteer Programs*, Volunteer Management Associates, Boulder, Colorado, 9th edit, 1988.

Books on the management of volunteers are few. Opinion and advice is readily available in articles, information sheets, guidelines and resource packs from the following organisations:

The Association of Independent Museums (AIM); The Volunteer Centre, UK; The National Council for Voluntary Organisations (NCVO); The British Association of Friends in Museums (BAFM); The Museums Association (MA).

A full bibliography prepared during the course of research for this publication is available from:

The Advisory Team,
The Volunteer Centre UK,
29 Lower King's Road,
Berkhamsted,
Hertfordshire, HP4 2AB.

Telephone: 0442 873311
Fax: 0442 870852.

Acronyms

AAMV	American Association of Museum Volunteers
ABSA	Association of Business Sponsorship of the Arts
ACE	Action for Children's Education
AIM	Association of Independent Museums
BAFM	British Association of Friends of Museums
CAB	Citizens Advice Bureau
CANS	Citizens Advice Notes Service
CMSU	Cheshire Museums Services Unit
CPSA	Civil and Public Services Association
CSU	Civil Service Union
DSS	Department of Social Security
EMAMS	East Midlands Area Museums Service
FDA	Association of First Division Civil Servants
GAGMA	Glasgow Art Gallery and Museums Association
IPMS	Institution of Professional Managers and Specialists
LIVE	Learn Through International Volunteering Effort
MA	Museums Association
MDA	Museum Documentation Association
MTI	Museums Training Institute
NADFAS	National Association of Decorative & Fine Arts Associations
NALGO	National and Local Government Officers' Union
NCVO	National Council for Voluntary Organisations
NOMU	National Organisations Management Unit
NUPE	National Union of Public Employees
NWMS	North West Museums Services
REACH	Retired Executives Action Clearing House
UKIC	United Kingdom Institute for Conservation
VAMI	Voluntari Associati per I Musei Italiani
VCAM	Volunteer Committee of Art Museums in USA and Canada
VCC	Voluntary Conservation Corp
VC(UK)	Volunteer Centre UK
WFFM	World Federation of Friends of Museums

INDEX

106

job guidance, 64

Keene, Suzanne, 25
Kelly, Barbara, 17, 25
Kew Bridge Steam Engine, 19

Lady Wood Bridge, 8
liabilities, 65, 71–2; *s.a.* employment law
libraries in museums and galleries, c. sts. 1 (78–9), 2 (79–80), 4 (81–3)
Library and Information Unit, The, (NCVO), 99
Local Authority Support for Museums, the Arts, Cultural Activities & Entertainments (Audit Commission), 11
local communities, using museums, 29
Local Development Agencies, 99
Local Government & Housing Act, The, (1989), 11

MA, 101
management, 5, 11–12; general organisation, 11–17; legal obligations, 48–53; policies for vol's 27–34; recruitment, 35; & staff relations, 62–66; & support services, 98–9; & training, 43–4; App I, 74–7; all c. sts. (78–90); *s.a.* employment law
Management Development Unit, The, 44
managers *see* management, vol'r co-ordinator
Managing Volunteers in Museums (Smith, S.B.), 25
Manchester Jewish Museum, The, 21, 40
Manpower Services Commission, The, 6
Manual of Curatorship (ed. Thompson), 25
manuals, for vol's *see* handbooks
Mary Rose Trust, The (Portsmouth), 20
Massachusetts Institute of Technology, The, c. st. 9 (89–90)
Mattingly, Jenny, 11, 25; - - Report, 66
MDA, 18, 93, c. st. 6 (84–5)
Merseyside Maritime Museum, The, 12, 13, 15, 20, App I, 74
Mid-Gloucester Engine Preservation Society, The, 19–20
Milan Cathedral, 22
Miles Report, The (Museums in Scotland) (HMSO), 7, 25
monitoring *see* evaluation
motivation of vol's, 43, (checklist), 45–6
motives, for volunteering, 21, 43, 70
MTI, 93
Museum of London, The, 16
Museum of Science & Industry, The (Manchester), 12, 14, App I, 75, c. st. 3 (80–81)
Museum of South Somerset, The, 10
Museum Professional Training & Career Structure (Hale Report), 22, 26
Museum Projects: A Handbook for Volunteers (Tanner), c. st. 5 (83–4)
Museum Quarterly, The (art: Worts), 26
Museum Registration Scheme, The, 9–10, 17, c. st. 7 (85–6)
Museum Training Institute, The, 71
Museums and Galleries Commission, The, 6, 9, 12, 17, 25; *s.a.* curators, supervision
Museums Association, The, 9, 17, 44, 71, report by, 14

staff relations, 13–15, 17; guidelines for, 29, 44–7, 62–9; special problems, 62–3, 97; c. st. 8 (86–8)

status, of museums, 7–8, 11–12, App I, 74–7

Storer, J.D. 25

student workers, in museums, 22, c. sts. 1 (78–9), 3 (80–81), 6 (84–5); *s.a.* internships

supervision, of vol's, 11–12, 18–19, 71, c. st. 6 (84–5)

support groups, for museums, App I, 74–7, App III, 91–9, all c. sts. (78–90), *s.a.* Friends

Tanner, Kathy, c. st. 5 (83–4)

Tate Gallery, The (London), 14, 20, App I, 74

Tax and Notional Earning Position of Volunteers (VC), 98

taxation, of vol's, 9, 58, *s.a.* employment law

TGWU, 66

Third Sector, in museums, 6

time commitment, by vol's, 9, 71–2, App I, 74–7

Torfaen Museum Trust (Ponytpool), 11

tourists, using museums, 8, 11

Trade Union Congress, 67

Trade Unions, and vol's in Italy, 94; in policy planning, 15, 29; and staff relations, 63, 66–8, 76

training, of vol's, 10, 16–17; as guides, 20–21; in-service provision, 43–4; in Italy, 94; by NADFAS, 43; *s.a.* App I, 74–7, App III, 91–9, internships, VC(UK), NCVO, all c. sts. (78–90)

Tramway Museum Society, The, c. st. 4 (81–3)

trusts, serving museums, 7, 9, 11; & policy planning, 27–35; *s.a.* Friends

types, of museums, 5–11; *s.a.* status

UKIC, 92

UK Volunteering Forum, The, 98

undergraduates, as vol's, 15; *s.a.* student

unemployed, the, as vol's, 85

UNESCO World Heritage Site, 8

United States of America, 14, 20, 95–7, ethnic groups in, 40, taxation in, 9, 61, c. sts. 8 (86–8), 9 (89–90)

University of East Anglia, The, 16, 20

Urban Programme, The, 8

Vale and Downland Museum, The (Wantage), 75

VAMI, 23, 91, full report, 93–5

VCAM, 91

VCC, 91

Victoria and Albert Museum, The, (London), 12, 14, 22, App I, 74, c. st. 1 (78–9)

VOLNET UK, 98

Volunteer Agencies Directory (NCVO), 99

volunteer activities, *Administrative*: administration, 16, 93; car-park, 16; catering, 23, App I, 74–7, c. st. 3 (80–81); cleaning, 19, 93, c. sts. 3 (80–81), 7 (85–6); education, 14, 16, 20, 93, App I, 74–4, c. st. 9 (89–90); exhibition work, 8, App I, c. sts. 7, 9; fund-raising, 72, App I, 74–5; information services, 11, 12, 23, 32, App I, 76, c. st. 1 (78–9), 8 (86–8); management, 65–6, c. st. 3 (80–81), App I, 74–7; outreach, c. st. 2 (79–80); publicity, App I, 74–7; security, 14, App I, 74–7, c. st. 7; *Clerical*: archives, 14; cataloguing, 14, 93, c. sts. 2 (79–80), 6 (84–5), 8 (86–8); clerical, App I, 74–7, c. st. 7 (85–6); computerisation, 12, c. st. 5 (83–4); documentation, 10, 11, 12, 32, App I, 74–7, c. sts. 5 (83–4), 6 (84–5), 7 (85–6); filing, 14, c. st. 8 (86–8); indexing,

Notes:

App   =   Appendix

art   =   Article

c. st.   =   Case Study

s.a.   =   see also

vol'r   =   volunteer